ACCLAIM FOR

PALESTINIANS AND ISRAELIS: A SHORT HISTORY OF CONFLICT

"This book is both necessary and accessible. So many people are mystified by this never-ending Middle East conflict. Here at last is a concise and readable account of a fundamental international issue of our time, one that has implications far beyond the region where it is set."

Jon Snow, journalist and broadcaster, UK

"Michael Scott-Baumann makes the complexities of the Israeli-Palestinian conflict easy to understand in this clear, straightforward and unemotional history."

John McHugo, author of *A Concise History of the Arabs*

"Excellent ... the ideal introduction to the history of the conflict between Israel and the Palestinians. A masterpiece of clarity, concision and balance, and written in a lively and accessible style, it provides a lucid overview of all key aspects of this complex and extremely important story. Scott-Baumann writes with great sensitivity and insight, enabling his readers to understand the perspectives of different historical actors, and to grasp the essence of competing interpretations of key events ... This book should be thrust into the hands of all those in need of a brief, clear and approachable account of the historical background to this still unresolved and geopolitically critical conflict."

Adam Sutcliffe, professor of European history at King's College and coeditor of *The Cambridge History of Judai* ·· · ····

"It is a high-risk venture to attempt an impartial account of the process, enabled by the British, by which the Jews gained a state in Palestine and the indigenous Palestinian Arabs were denied one. Scott-Baumann has taken that risk and succeeded with as near as it comes to a textbook history that brings us up to date with the injustice and dispossession that inform Israel and Palestine."

Tim Llewellyn, former BBC Middle East correspondent

"Scott-Baumann set himself the difficult challenge of writing a primer on the now over-a-century-long history of one of the most complex conflicts of modern times. Not only does he rise to the challenge, but he even manages to offer insights that go beyond conventional historical accounts."

Gilbert Achcar, author of *The Arabs and the Holocaust*

"A complete history exploring the conflict between Israel and Palestine in just a few hundred pages … A useful reference."

School Library Journal

"The huge library on the conflict and the massive information it contains requires that authors write books that effectively transmit that knowledge to a wide public. Now comes Michael Scott-Baumann, who does just this excellently. His thirty-five years' experience as a teacher and lecturer in history is felt on each page of his book … A road map to students and an entrance gate to whomever wants to go beyond it."

Menachem Klein, professor of political science at Bar-Ilan University and author of *Lives in Common*

MICHAEL SCOTT-BAUMANN

PALESTINIANS AND ISRAELIS

A SHORT HISTORY OF CONFLICT

First published 2021
This updated edition published 2023

The History Press
97 St George's Place, Cheltenham,
Gloucestershire, GL50 3QB
www.thehistorypress.co.uk

Published in North America in revised and updated form by The Experiment,
LLC, in 2023 as *The Shortest History of Israel and Palestine: From Zionism to
Intifadas and the Struggle for Peace*

British Library Cataloguing in Publication Data.
A catalogue record for this book is available from the British Library.

ISBN 978 1 80399 676 9

Printed and bound in Great Britain by TJ Books Limited, Padstow, Cornwall.

Trees for LYfe

Contents

Preface

The Israeli-Palestinian conflict has existed for three-quarters of a century. In essence it is a dispute over land, the land of Palestine, and includes what is today the State of Israel together with the West Bank and Gaza. It is a relatively small area of land, not much larger than Belgium or the state of Maryland, and its population is no more than thirteen million. The conflict is a dispute between Jewish immigrants and their descendants who have followed the ideology of Zionism and the Palestinian Arabs among whom the Zionists settled. Both claim the right to live in, and control, some or all of Palestine.

This book provides an up-to-date, historical account both for the student and the general reader who follows news of the ongoing conflict yet struggles to understand how it originated and has developed over the last century. It comes in the wake of former president Donald Trump's "Deal of the Century," Israeli threats to annex Palestinian land on the West Bank, and the eruption of violence across Israel and Palestine in May 2021.

The book outlines the pre-1914 origins of the conflict before examining Britain's role in the interwar development of the embryonic Jewish state and the Jewish-Arab tension that accompanied it. Above all, it explains the unique circumstances in which the State of Israel was created and examines both Israeli and Palestinian narratives of those events. It shows how history has shaped the present and continues to influence policy. In examining a century of rapid change, it identifies key turning points, but it also highlights the elements of continuity, the links between the past and the present.

While explaining the context of the wider Arab-Israeli conflict, the book focuses on the struggle between Israelis and Palestinians. Thus, the second half of the book explores the development of the Israeli occupation of the Palestinian territories, and resistance to it, which is at the heart of the Israeli-Palestinian conflict today, as well as the challenges of peacemaking.

Each chapter starts with the key questions to be answered and ends by illuminating the human impact of the conflict with the inclusion of personal testimony, from an Israeli or a Palestinian perspective, using sources such as diaries, interviews, memoirs, and newspaper reports.

Throughout, maps show how boundaries have changed over the course of the last century, and a timeline of significant dates is included on pages 3 to 5. Key terms are set in bold, elucidated in the text, and further explained in a glossary at the end of the book. Here, you will also find brief biographical sketches of the key players, whose names are also in bold type.

Chronology

1945	Arab League formed
1946	King David Hotel bombing in Jerusalem
1947	SS *Exodus* refugee ship prevented from landing in Palestine
	United Nations votes for the partition of Palestine
	Start of civil war in Palestine
1948	Declaration of the new State of Israel
1948–49	First Arab-Israeli War
1948	United Nations Relief and Works Agency (UNRWA) established
	UN Resolution 194 recognising Palestinians' right to return
1950	Israel passes Law of Absentees' Property
	Israeli Law of Return allows any Jew to become a citizen of Israel
1955	Operation Black Arrow
1956	Suez Crisis
1959	Fatah formally established
1964	Palestine Liberation Organization (PLO) founded
1967	Six-Day War
	UN Resolution 242
1968	Battle of Karameh
1969	Yasser Arafat becomes chairman of the PLO
1970	PLO expelled from Jordan
1972	Munich Olympics massacre
1973	Yom Kippur War
1974	Arafat speech to UN
	Gush Emunim founded
1977	Likud Government formed in Israel
1979	Egypt-Israel peace treaty
1982	Israeli invasion of Lebanon
	Palestinians massacred in the Sabra and Shatila refugee camps

1987	Start of the First Palestinian Intifada
1993, 1995	Oslo Accords
1995	Assassination of Yitzhak Rabin
2000	Camp David peace negotiations
	Start of the Second Intifada
2001	9/11 attacks on the United States
	Start of Hamas suicide bombings
2002	Israeli "Operation Defensive Shield" in occupied territories
2003	President George W. Bush releases the "Roadmap for Peace"
2004	Death of Yasser Arafat
2005	Israeli evacuation of Gaza
2006	Hamas victory in Palestinian elections
2008	War in Gaza
2009	Benjamin Netanyahu elected prime minister
2014	War in Gaza
2018	Israel passes the Nation-State Law
2020	President Donald J. Trump announces the "Deal of the Century"
2021	Upsurge in violence in East Jerusalem and Gaza
	Netanyahu replaced as prime minister
2022	Killing of Shireen Abu Aklah, Palestinian American journalist
	Netanyahu reelected as prime minister
2023	October 7: Hamas attack on Israel kills more than 1,300 people and takes more than 150 hostages
	October 8: Israel formally declares war on Hamas
	Israel's retaliatory bombardment of Gaza kills more than 2,600 people in the following week

CHAPTER 1

The Origins of the Conflict

- Why did European Jews migrate to Palestine?
- What was the impact of Zionism on the Arabs in Palestine?

Palestine before the First World War

The land of Palestine, a strip of land between the Jordan River and the Mediterranean Sea, was conquered by Arab Muslims in the seventh century following the emergence of the religion of Islam in what today is Saudi Arabia. Over time, most of the population adopted Arabic as its language and Islam as its religion, although a substantial Christian community and a small Jewish one remained. Then, in the sixteenth century, Palestine was conquered by the **Ottomans** (a Turkish dynasty named after its founder, Osman). The Ottomans were Muslims but not Arab speaking. They went on to conquer most of the Arab lands of the Middle East and thus came into possession of the three most holy sites for Muslims: Mecca, Medina, and Jerusalem.

In the Ottoman Middle East, there was no officially designated area called "Palestine," as such. Instead, the area to the west of the Jordan River and south of Beirut made up the three administrative districts of Jerusalem, Nablus, and Acre. However, the region was generally referred to as Palestine (***Filastin*** in Arabic).

The population of late nineteenth-century Palestine was 85 percent Muslim and about 10 percent Christian. It was

A family of Arab fellahin, or peasant, farmers

largely rural and most of the population were *fellahin*, or peasant farmers. Palestinian society and politics were dominated by a small number of urban families. These "notables," as they were often referred to, were landowners, often with commercial interests. They acted as intermediaries between the Ottoman government and the local population. Some were elected as members of the Ottoman parliament in Istanbul, the capital of the Ottoman Empire. Many held senior government posts and religious positions. They collected taxes for the Ottoman authorities.

In the late nineteenth century, Palestine came into increasing contact with European traders and its farmers began to grow more cotton, cereals, olives, and oranges for export. The port city of Jaffa increased the value of its agricultural exports from roughly $120,000 in 1850 to $1,875,000 by 1914 and its population quadrupled in size between 1880 and 1914.[1] It was not only trade that brought Palestine into closer contact with the European world: increasing numbers of Christian pilgrims came by steamship to visit the biblical sites of the Holy Land. They contributed funds for church building and stimulated the development of a tourist industry.

Most Palestinian Arabs were loyal to the Ottoman state, participating in elections to the parliament in Istanbul and in local government, as well as sending their children to the growing number of state schools. However, a change of government in Istanbul in 1908 led to insistence on the use of Turkish, as opposed to Arabic, in schools, law courts, and government offices in Palestine. This aroused criticism in Palestine's Arabic press and contributed to the emergence of a nascent Arab nationalism. Yet it was the issue of Jewish immigration that increasingly exercised Arab opinion in Palestine and led to calls for preventive action by the Ottoman government.

Zionism and Jewish Communities in Palestine

The Jews had lived in what is today Israel and Palestine from about 1500 BCE. In 64 BCE the Romans conquered Jerusalem and Palestine became part of the Roman Empire. Then, in 135 CE, after a series of revolts against Roman imperial rule, the Jews were finally dispersed. A minority remained but the majority settled in Europe and other parts of the Arab world.

By the late nineteenth century, most Jews lived in the European parts of the Russian Empire. Many were forced to live in specially designated areas in the Russian Pale of Settlement and were subject to severe restrictions, the result of a policy designed to exclude them from the life of Christians in the Russian Empire. After the assassination of the

A print of an attack on a Jew in late nineteenth-century Russia

Russian Tsar Alexander II in 1881, for which the Jews were widely blamed, a series of pogroms, officially approved riots, and campaigns of persecution were launched. Jews increasingly became the targets of **anti-Semitism**, verbal and often physical abuse directed at them because they were Jews. This experience had the effect of strengthening the belief among many Jews that they shared an identity, history, and culture, regardless of whether they were religiously observant or not. But it also persuaded many to flee. Between 1882 and 1914, 2.5 million Jews left Russia, the vast majority to the US and Europe to the west of Russia. However, a small number, about fifty-five thousand, made their way to Palestine, their ancestral home.

Jews had dreamed of returning to *Eretz* **Israel**, the biblical "Land of Israel," and had prayed for "Next Year in Jerusalem" for hundreds of years. Now, especially with the development of the steamship in the nineteenth century, it became a more practical proposition for some of them.

Those who emigrated to Palestine were motivated by the desire to escape persecution and find a safe haven, but, for many, that wish was combined with a desire for a national homeland.

Palestine had been home to a small number of Jews for hundreds of years, half of them living in Jerusalem, largely in harmony with their Palestinian Arab neighbours. They were made up of both Sephardic and **Ashkenazi Jews**. The former, mostly considered to be the descendants of Jews from Spain and North Africa, were predominantly Arabic speaking and some held positions in the Ottoman government. The latter had often come from Europe in preceding decades and tended to speak Yiddish (the language of most Eastern European Jews, derived primarily from German and Hebrew). Most of these so-called Ottoman Jews living in Palestine, whether Sephardic or Ashkenazi, were highly religious and eager to preserve and develop their Jewish identity within the Ottoman Empire. In contrast with those who were fleeing Russia, very few sought a separate, national homeland, let alone an independent Jewish state.

The Jewish settlers who arrived in the First **Aliyah** (Hebrew for "ascent") from 1882 onward were mostly farmers. Many found their new life very harsh and departed after a short time, usually to Western Europe or the US, while those who acquired land and survived often only managed to do so with the help of cheap Arab labour. Although most of the settlers who arrived in the 1880s came from Russia, particularly from what is present-day Poland, their ideology and political organisation, and that of their supporters, was to be formulated not by a Russian Jew but one from Vienna.

Theodor Herzl, a lawyer and journalist, wrote a book titled *The Jewish State*, which was published in 1896. He called for the Jews to form a single nation-state like that of France or Germany. Echoing the sentiments of other European colonisers at the time, he claimed that the Jewish state

Theodor Herzl

could also be an "an outpost of civilization," a defence against the perceived barbarism of "Asia."[2]

In 1897, Herzl organised a congress in Switzerland in which the **World Zionist Organization (WZO)** was formed. Though it was not the first time that the term had been used, the delegates at the congress now defined **Zionism** as the belief in "the creation of a home for the Jewish people in Palestine."[3] Herzl's political priority was to secure the diplomatic support of a great power in Europe and financial backing from European and American Jewry, some of whose members had acquired considerable wealth. The **Jewish National Fund (JNF)** was set up in 1901 to buy land in Palestine. Today, most of the land of Israel is held in trust for the world's Jews by the JNF. It cannot be sold to non-Jews.

The Jewish immigrants of the Second Aliyah from 1904 onward also came mostly from the Polish lands of the Russian Empire. However, they were much more ideologically driven, and keen to implement Herzl's ideas. After centuries of persecution, they stressed the importance of using the biblical language of Hebrew as a sign of their rebirth in what they saw as their Jewish homeland. Many of them displayed the characteristics of the pioneer – tough and self-reliant – and were determined to show how different they were from the image of the weak, helpless Jews of the Russian Pale. They developed the concepts of the **Conquest of Land** and the **Conquest of Labor**.

The Conquest of Land emphasised the importance of colonizing, irrigating, and cultivating the land. The Conquest of Labor articulated the belief that the Jews' rebirth as a nation was best achieved through becoming economically independent and reliant on Jewish-only labour.

Many Jews living in Jerusalem, especially those who had been resident for many generations, were far from enthusiastic. Similarly, only a minority of Jews in Europe supported the Zionist project: for example, the more assimilated ones feared that their loyalty to the states in which they lived might be questioned and that the Zionist project would make Jews less welcome to stay in Europe.

Arabs and Jews in Palestine – Neighbours or Enemies?

Many Zionists, especially those living abroad, believed that Palestine was, in the words made famous by the writer Israel Zangwill, "a land without a people for a people without a land."[4] Or, at the very least, that it was a desolate, sparsely populated country.

Large areas were, indeed, thinly populated, particularly in the desert regions of the south. However, as many early Jewish settlers acknowledged, much of its land was cultivated and many of its Arab inhabitants were opposed to Jewish settlement. As early as 1899, Yusuf Diya al-Khalidi, a former mayor of Jerusalem, sent a message to Theodore Herzl in which he recognised the historic rights of Jews in Palestine but pleaded, "In the name of God, let Palestine be left alone."[5] Herzl replied that Jewish settlers intended no harm and that Jewish wealth would bring benefits.

In the early years of Jewish settlement, some Arabs did, undoubtedly, gain jobs and income working on Jewish farms and in Jewish businesses. But many Arab tenant farmers were evicted from the land they had worked for generations after their Arab landowners, often absentees living in cities like Jerusalem or Beirut, sold it to Jewish newcomers. The farmers' cause was taken up by the Arabic press: the newspaper *Filastin* appealed to fellow Arabs not to sell land to Jewish immigrants. Increasing reference was made, both in the press and by notables, to the terms "Palestine" and "Palestinian." A sense of Palestinian identity was coming to be shared by an increasing number of Palestinian Arabs.

Some Jews employed Arabs to work on the farms, plantations, and in factories they owned and some of them lived in mixed, Jewish and Arab, neighbourhoods. They saw themselves not as foreign colonisers but as people "returning" to their homeland, hoping to live in harmony with their Arab neighbours. However, many of the more recent immigrants of the Second Aliyah were determined to live and work separately. They wished to replace Arab labourers with Jewish ones, even if they were less skillful and had to be paid higher wages. For them, "Hebrew labor" was more important than economic efficiency. Furthermore, the WZO was prepared to subsidise them with funds channeled through the JNF.

Fear of eviction and dispossession undoubtedly fueled the growth of anti-Zionist sentiment in Palestine. Urban notables and the Arabic press called on the Ottoman government to halt immigration and land purchases, and, occasionally, restrictions were imposed by the Ottoman authorities in Palestine. However, immigration and settlement activity intensified in the early twentieth century, and in 1907, the WZO founded the Palestine Office in Jaffa to coordinate land purchase and organise the building of Jewish settlements.

The institutional foundations of the *Yishuv*, as the Jewish community in Palestine was known, were laid in the decades leading up to the outbreak of war in 1914. Yet the Jewish population, at about seventy-five thousand, still only made up about 7 percent of the population, and not all were Zionists.

Few Arabs came into direct contact with Jewish colonists. However, there was friction, sometimes violence, in and around Jewish settlements. Disputes over land led to attacks on Jewish property, and fighting resulted in a small but increasing number of fatalities.

By 1914, two emerging national communities were beginning to collide in their desire for the same land. The Arabs sought to maintain their position as the owners, while the Zionists sought to buy as much land as possible and turn it into a Jewish homeland.

When the First World War ended, in 1918, the Ottoman Empire, and its rule over Palestine, had collapsed. Another major power was to have a far more decisive impact on both the Arab and the Jewish communities in Palestine.

Personal Testimony

A Late Nineteenth-Century Jewish Immigrant

Herbert Bentwich was an unusual Zionist. Most Zionist immigrants were poor Eastern Europeans fleeing from persecution in Tsarist Russia. Bentwich, however, was an affluent British Jew of the professional class.

His great-grandson, Ari Shavit, an Israeli citizen, has read his great-grandfather's memoirs. Shavit wonders why his ancestor "does not see the land as it is," and he strives to understand why his great-grandfather is oblivious of the Arab villages:

> Riding in the elegant carriage from Jaffa to Mikveh Yisrael, he did not see the Palestinian village of Abu Kabir. Traveling from Mikveh Yisrael to Rishon LeZion, he did not see the Palestinian village of Yazur. On his way from Rishon LeZion to Ramleh he did not see the Palestinian village of Sarafand. And in Ramleh he did not really see that Ramleh is a Palestinian town. Now, standing atop the white tower, he does not see the nearby Palestinian town of Lydda …
>
> How is it possible that my great-grandfather does not see?
>
> There are more than half a million Arabs, Bedouins, and Druze in Palestine in 1897. There are twenty cities and towns, and hundreds of villages. So how can the pedantic Bentwich not notice them? How can the hawk-eyed Bentwich not see from the tower of Ramleh that the Land

is taken? That there is another people now occupying the land of his ancestors?

I am not critical or judgmental. On the contrary, I realize that the Land of Israel on his mind is a vast hundred thousand square kilometers, which includes today's Kingdom of Jordan. And in this vast land there are fewer than a million inhabitants. There is enough room there for the Jewish survivors of anti-Semitic Europe. Greater Palestine can be home to both Jew and Arab ...

He might easily persuade himself that the Jews who will come from Europe will only better the lives of the local population, that European Jews will cure the natives, educate them, cultivate them. That they will live side by side with them in an honorable and dignified manner. But there is a far stronger argument: in April 1897 there is no Palestinian people. There is no real sense of Palestinian self-determination, and there is no Palestinian national movement to speak of ...

As I observe the blindness of Herbert Bentwich as he surveys the Land from the top of the tower, I understand him perfectly. My great-grandfather does not see because he is motivated by the need not to see. He does not see because if he does, he will have to turn back. But my great-grandfather cannot turn back. So that he can carry on, my great-grandfather chooses not to see.[6]

CHAPTER 2

The First World War and the British Mandate

After the First World War, Britain took control of and ruled Palestine.

- **Why was the Balfour Declaration of 1917 so significant?**
- **How did Britain govern Palestine under the mandate?**
- **How did the Jewish community in Palestine develop?**

Palestine in the First World War

In August 1914, Germany and Austria-Hungary (the Central Powers) went to war with Britain, France, and Russia (the Allies). Three months later, the Ottoman Empire joined the Central Powers. Thousands of Palestinian Arabs were drafted into the Ottoman Army. Most of them remained loyal to the Ottomans, even if wishing for greater autonomy within the Empire. Meanwhile, the Jewish community was cut off from Europe as the flow of immigrants and money dried up.

As the war continued, more and more Palestinian men were conscripted, and increased amounts of crops and cattle were seized to feed them. The rule of the Ottoman military governor in the region, Jamal Pasha, became increasingly harsh, particularly so after British troops took control of Sinai to the south and threatened Ottoman control of Palestine. Many of the politically active Palestinian Arabs, even if they were not working for an Ottoman defeat, were arrested and imprisoned. Some were deported and dozens executed. Yet there was no uprising against Ottoman rule, and many Palestinian Arabs, together with a small number of Jews, continued to fight in the Ottoman Army. In late 1917, the Ottoman forces in Palestine were defeated by the British, and in December 1917, General Edmund Allenby led his troops into Jerusalem. He promised as little disruption to "lawful business" as possible. However, the First World War was to end four hundred years of Ottoman rule in the Middle East and produce changes that are still felt, by both Arabs and Jews, in what is today Israel and Palestine.

British Intervention during the War

During the war, as it attempted to secure its strategic and geopolitical interests, Britain made a series of agreements that conflicted with and contradicted each other. Three significant agreements affected Palestine, yet British concern was primarily focused on winning the war, and the spoils of war, not about the people of Palestine.

The first of these agreements was made in 1915. It consisted of a series of letters exchanged by Henry McMahon, the British high commissioner in Egypt, and **Hussein, the sharif of Mecca** and the leader of the Hashemite Dynasty. Hussein was guardian of Mecca and Medina, the two most holy sites of Islam (in what is today Saudi Arabia), and he oversaw the annual hajj (or pilgrimage) to Mecca. As such, he was considered by many to be the most important Arab Muslim leader.

McMahon knew that Hussein was fearful of the Ottoman government encroaching on his power and he promised Hussein that if the Arabs fought against the Ottoman Army, the British would support "the independence of the Arab countries," on condition that the Arabs sought British advice about how to establish their government.

The British were eager to protect the Suez Canal, Britain's route to the oil of Persia (today's Iran) and to its empire in India, from any Ottoman or subsequent threat. An Arab army could help to allay British fears. When Hussein sought clarity on the issue of the borders of a new Arab state, McMahon was deliberately ambiguous about the status of Palestine and whether it was to be included in the new Arab state.[1]

Hussein was promised gold and guns by the British, and in 1916, an Arab army was raised and led by Emir (Prince) Faisal, Hussein's son. In what became known as the Arab Revolt, the army blew up Turkish trains, disrupted the flow of military supplies to the Turkish soldiers, and helped to push the Turks out of Jordan and Syria. The activities of this Arab army are well known, because an English Army intelligence officer, Major T. E. Lawrence, later known in Britain as "Lawrence of Arabia," fought with the Arabs.

Made in secret in 1916, the second agreement is known as the Sykes-Picot Agreement after the British and French politicians who signed it. They looked ahead to the eventual defeat of the Ottoman Empire and decided that the liberated Arab lands would be allocated to distinct French and British spheres of influence. In other words, the "independent" state that had been promised to Hussein (about which the French were kept in the dark) would be overlaid with some degree of European control. Syria, including what is today Lebanon, would go to the French, while the area from the Sinai to Mesopotamia (present-day Iraq) would go to the British. Most of Palestine, which both countries desired, was to be under some sort of international control.

When they found out about this deal at the end of the war, Arab leaders felt betrayed. Were they simply to exchange Ottoman for European masters? It seemed that Britain and France were determined to maintain and extend their power and influence in the Middle East and had decided to carve up the Arab lands between themselves.

The Balfour Declaration, 1917

The third agreement that the British made, and which proved to have the most far-reaching consequences of all, was the **Balfour Declaration** of November 1917. It took the form of a letter, written by the British Foreign Secretary, **Arthur Balfour**, to Lord Rothschild, a leading British Jew, in which he expressed support for a national home for the Jews in Palestine. The pledge made by the British government was only sixty-five words long:

> His Majesty's Government view with favour the establishment in Palestine of a national home for the Jewish people. The Government will make every effort to help bring this about. It is clearly understood that nothing shall be done which may harm the civil and religious rights of existing non-Jewish communities in Palestine, or the rights and political status enjoyed by Jews in any other country.

The British were very careful with the wording of the declaration. It affirmed their support for a Jewish homeland, a deliberately vague concept, not a state with its own borders and independent government. However, for the next thirty years, many Jews regarded the declaration as a promise from the British government to help set up a Jewish state. The declaration contained no sense of Palestine as an Arab land. The Arabs, who made up 90 percent of the population, were simply referred to as "non-Jewish communities" whose "civil and religious rights" were to be protected.

Why Did Britain Issue the Balfour Declaration?

The Balfour Declaration was, first and foremost, a product of the exigencies of war. When it was issued in November 1917, Britain was bogged down fighting on the Western Front. The United States had entered the First World War but, as yet, to little effect. In Russia, the faction of Communists known as Bolsheviks threatened to take power and drop out of the war. Some members of the British government thought that winning the support of influential Jews, whether American capitalists or Russian Bolsheviks, for the Allied cause might strengthen their commitment to the war effort. This view may have been based on an inflated assessment of the power of international Jewry. However, it was a view that **Chaim Weizmann**, the British leader of the WZO, was happy to cultivate in the minds of British policy makers if it led them to lend their support to the Zionist cause.

Such military and diplomatic considerations also shaped Britain's longer-term imperial thinking about the importance of Palestine. Palestine stood astride the overland route to the oil reserves of Iraq, and Britain was planning to build a pipeline from Iraq to the port of Haifa in Palestine, from where it could be shipped to Britain. Above all, Palestine was only a hundred miles north of the Suez Canal (see map on p. 26).

The Suez Canal was of huge commercial and strategic importance: it constituted the main route to India and Britain's other colonies in the Far East and was the route through which most of Britain's oil, now so vital for the navy, was transported. British control of Palestine, increasingly seen as preferable to the internationalisation envisaged in the Sykes-Picot Agreement of 1916, would provide a buffer zone. Many Cabinet members were persuaded that a significant Jewish entity in Palestine would constitute a reliable European ally in what they saw as a backward, corrupt, and volatile Arab world. Thus, support for Zionism was motivated by both wartime and longer-term imperial goals.

Strong Personalities

Religious beliefs also had some impact on Prime Minister David Lloyd George and Foreign Secretary Balfour. Both had come under the influence of C. P. Scott and of his close ally, Chaim Weizmann. Scott was editor of the *Manchester Guardian*, a newspaper of international renown, and Weizmann was the most prominent Zionist in Britain and later became first president of the State of Israel. During the war, Weizmann carried out important scientific research for the British government at the University

Chaim Weizmann

23

of Manchester. Both Scott and Weizmann appealed to the Christian Zionist in Lloyd George and Balfour and cited the biblical reasons, with which both men would have been familiar, for supporting a Jewish return to Palestine.[2]

The persuasive powers of Scott and Weizmann and, in particular, the charm and charisma of the latter ("an irresistible political seducer," according to the philosopher Sir Isaiah Berlin), were of considerable significance in convincing Balfour, Lloyd George, and other British leaders that British and Zionist interests in Palestine were closely aligned and that a growing Jewish population in Palestine would have every reason to be supportive of British interests. Religious or cultural views undoubtedly complemented more hardheaded political reasons for supporting the development of a more significant Jewish presence in Palestine.

Whatever the prime reasons for British policy, the Balfour Declaration, issued by the preeminent power in the Middle East at the end of the war, made the survival of the Zionist project far more likely.

The British Mandate for Palestine

Weizmann headed the Zionist delegation at the postwar Paris Peace Conference, determined to ensure the declaration was incorporated into the peace settlement. When asked what was meant by a Jewish national home, he replied, "To make Palestine as Jewish as England is English." However, he was careful not to speak openly of a Jewish "state," so as not to be accused of trying to make the Jewish minority become the masters of the Arab majority. He knew there was a limit to how far he could push the British. As president of the WZO, he was aware that if the Jewish national home was to survive it needed the continued support of the British.

Balfour himself did not need much persuading. In fact, he was explicit in dismissing any concern for the interests of the "non-Jewish communities" in Palestine. In the summer of 1919, he said, "We are dealing not with the wishes of an existing community but are consciously seeking to reconstitute a new community and definitely building for a numerical [Jewish] majority in the future," and in a note to Lord Curzon, his successor as foreign secretary, he wrote that Zionism was "of far profounder import than the desires and prejudices of the 700,000 Arabs who now inhabit that ancient land" and Arab claims to Palestine were "infinitely weaker than those of the Jews."[3]

In 1920, at an international conference in San Remo, in Italy, both Britain and France acquired **mandates** over the Arab lands that were taken from the defeated Ottomans. This meant that the European powers were ordered "to govern until such time as they [the Arab countries] are able to stand alone." France was given control of Syria and Lebanon, and Britain was allocated Iraq, Palestine, and what became known as Transjordan.

The awards were formally recognised by the League of Nations in 1923. Under Article 22 of the League's Covenant, the mandatory powers, Britain and France, were responsible for preparing the countries for self-government. The well-being and development of those peoples was to form "a sacred trust of civilisation." This meant preparing the peoples of the mandated territories for independence.

In the case of Palestine, the Balfour Declaration was written into the British Mandate, and it was made even more explicitly pro-Zionist: the British were authorised to liaise with a "Jewish Agency," a body representing the Jewish

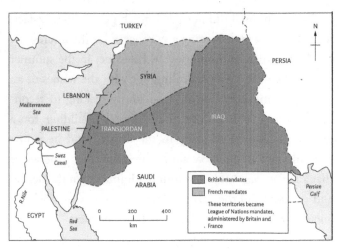

The Middle East after the First World War

community in Palestine (and not with a corresponding Arab one); to "facilitate Jewish immigration"; and to encourage the "close settlement by Jews on the land." Yet again, "the civil and religious rights of all the inhabitants of Palestine" were to be safeguarded but there was no reference to the Arabs as a people or any explicit acknowledgement of their right to self-determination. For Palestinian Arabs, the mandate was colonial rule in its crudest form, only under a new guise.

Under the League of Nations mandate, Britain was given responsibility for "the development of self-governing institutions," yet the colonial secretary, Winston Churchill, made it clear in 1921 that no representative bodies would be permitted in Palestine if they interfered with the idea of a "Jewish national home." In other words, self-government would only be granted if the Arabs accepted the Balfour Declaration. This they refused to do.

When Britain offered an elected, legislative assembly to the Arabs in 1922 and 1928, the British did not propose to grant them the majority of seats, which their numerical preponderance warranted, because this might enable them to exercise control over Zionist immigration and land purchase. Not surprisingly, the Arabs declined the offer of an assembly in which their powers would be so circumscribed. According to the historian Martin Gilbert, the "centrepiece of British Mandatory policy was the withholding of representative institutions in Palestine as long as there was an Arab majority."[4]

Throughout the 1920s the British government officially reassured the Palestinian Arabs that they, the British, had no intention of allowing the creation of a Jewish state in Palestine. The first high commissioner (head of the British administration) in Palestine, **Sir Herbert Samuel**, said that Britain had never consented and "would never consent" to the establishment of a Jewish government in Palestine. In March 1921, Churchill assured an Arab delegation that a Jewish national home would enable the Arabs to "share in the benefits and progress of Zionism," bringing an influx of capital and promoting economic development. Nevertheless, he was categorical in telling them, "You ask me to repudiate the Balfour Declaration and to stop immigration. This is not in my power, and it is not my wish."[5]

In Palestine itself, British officials and military personnel were often highly critical of government policy. After Arab-Jewish riots in 1920, in which 200 Jews and 120 Arabs were left dead or wounded, the British Court of Inquiry was unequivocal in its judgment: the Balfour Declaration was "undoubtedly the starting point of the whole trouble."[6] Yet British personnel continued to find their hands tied by the Balfour Declaration and were repeatedly told that it was a binding commitment.

Sir Herbert Samuel was a convinced and ardent Zionist who also attempted to be an evenhanded administrator. He strove to reconcile the Arab notables to British rule. After further riots in 1921, he suspended immigration temporarily and, when it was permitted again a month later, he announced that it would be limited by the "economic absorptive capacity"

Haj Amin al-Husseini

of Palestine and by "the interests of the present population."[7] This was undoubtedly a concession to the Arabs.

In 1922, Samuel established the **Supreme Muslim Council (SMC)** and helped to appoint **Haj Amin al-Husseini**, a member of one of Jerusalem's leading families, as its head. The SMC was granted control over extensive Muslim funds and property, including schools and religious courts. With a huge network of patronage at his disposal, al-Husseini became the most important Arab political figure and, as intended by Samuel, the main intermediary between the British and the Muslim community.

Nevertheless, the terms of the mandate and the way it was interpreted undoubtedly gave Jews a privileged position. Samuel never contemplated granting Arab majority rule because it would threaten continued immigration and the development of the Jewish National Home to which the British government remained committed. Not surprisingly, Jews had easier access to the British administration and held far more senior posts, relative to their population, in the government of Palestine.

The British contributed significantly to the economic development of Palestine, building railways, roads, schools, and public health services, and granted concessions, particularly to Jewish-owned companies, for certain projects. The foremost example of the latter was that given to the Russian-Jewish industrialist Pinchas Rutenberg, who built the electricity grid that supplied power to coastal towns, Jewish settlements, British military bases, and later to other parts of Palestine.

The Development of the Jewish Community in Palestine

In 1920, Jews still only made up 10 percent of the population of Palestine. Large-scale immigration was seen as vital to the survival of the *Yishuv*, the Jewish community in Palestine, and of the development of a Jewish National Home. Yet, by the end of the decade, only a hundred thousand Jews had migrated to Palestine. In 1927 and 1928, more emigrated than immigrated. For most migrating Jews, the United States and Western Europe remained more attractive destinations, while lack of funds for the development of Jewish farms and industrial enterprises sometimes hampered development in Palestine. Furthermore, not all Jews in Palestine were Zionists. Many members of the Old *Yishuv*, some of whom had lived on the land for centuries, lived and worked alongside the Arabs, especially in Jerusalem, and were far from committed to the idea of a national homeland, let alone desirous of being part of a Jewish state. Similarly, many recent immigrants from Eastern Europe had not necessarily come to be part of a Jewish nation, but rather to find a better life in Palestine.

Nevertheless, in the early years of the mandate, great strides were made in the development of the Jewish national community. For a start, the Zionist leaders had one clear goal: to build the foundations of a Jewish state in Palestine. To this end, two institutions took on the main responsibility: the **Jewish Agency** and the **Histadrut**.

The Jewish Agency represented and was, in practice, the government of the Jewish population in Palestine. It liaised with the British government on behalf of the Jewish community and controlled and oversaw the funding of settlement building. The Histadrut, the Zionist labour federation, was established in 1920 to promote Jewish workers. It not only organised and protected Jewish labour, it also set up social welfare programs for healthcare, housing, and, above all, the schools in which the Hebrew-speaking nation would be molded. It was financed by donations from international Jewry as well as by subscriptions that most Jews in Palestine paid in order to gain access to its services. After a series of Arab attacks on rural Jewish settlements in 1920–21, Histadrut also formed its own military force, the **Haganah** (later the basis of the Israeli Army).

In 1921, **David Ben-Gurion** became head of the Histadrut. He had come from Poland to Palestine, at the age of twenty, in 1906. Like many Zionists, he initially held that the Palestinian Arabs did not form a separate, national body but were part of a larger Arab nation. However, with the establishment of the British Mandate and the prospect of increased Jewish immigration, he acknowledged the strength of Palestinian national feeling: "We, as a nation, want this country to be ours; the Arabs, as a nation, want this country to be theirs."[8] While the Jews remained a minority in Palestine, they would continue to feel vulnerable. Ben-Gurion, like Weizmann, believed that the success of the Zionist project therefore depended on the continuing support, and protection, of the British.

An ardent socialist, Ben-Gurion was committed to the development of Jewish **kibbutzim**. Heavily subsidised by the WZO, the kibbutzim were cooperative farms in which work and living quarters were shared. Although more Jews lived in towns than in the countryside, it was the younger Jews who worked on the land,

David Ben-Gurion, who became head of the Jewish Agency in 1935

drained the marshes, and built the roads who became known as national heroes. The **sabra** generation, named after the cactus that is native to Palestine, were portrayed as tough, brave, and, above all, in touch with the land they farmed.

Ben-Gurion dominated the *Yishuv* in the interwar years. He became head of the Jewish Agency in 1935 and, in 1948, the first prime minister of Israel. Members of the Second Aliyah, who, like Ben-Gurion, had mostly come from Eastern Europe, were to dominate the leadership of the *Yishuv* and the State of Israel until the 1970s. Although a socialist, Ben-Gurion and his colleagues placed national interests above considerations of class, in line with the Zionist beliefs that held sway from the 1920s. In 1930, the Histadrut absorbed the two main political parties to form **Mapai**, the Workers' Party, which was later to form the basis of the **Israeli Labor Party**. Meanwhile, Histadrut formed the core, along with the Jewish Agency, of a centralised political and economic infrastructure and, in doing so, formed the foundations of a viable Jewish state.

My name is Israel. I am 20.

Good people died that I might be born in a land called home.

I have heard the stories and seen the graves.

But now we are here, and the land is ours. Not all milk and honey, but ours. We share a name, the land and I— Israel. And we share a birthday.

Twenty years, for me, a long time. For my people, who waited thousands of years, almost nothing.

But we have made something of that nothing.

Now the hills of rock are hills of trees. Fifty million trees, Jerusalem pines, planted one at a time.

Cities thrive where nothing thrived. Orange trees bloom where nothing bloomed.

An almost dead language is alive again. We read the Dead Sea Scrolls as easily as you read this magazine.

We mine copper where King Solomon mined copper.

We make fresh water from the sea,

and we share what we have learned with other nations.

We build airports and schools in Asia, sell baby chickens and farm equipment in Europe, and exchange our students with even younger countries in Africa.

How do we go to so many places? Easy. We have our own airline. El Al Israel Airlines.

You don't know what El Al means? It means "to the skies" in that almost dead language.

It also means that our jets are welcome in 17 different nations.

Yes, we have everything now: Universities, symphony orchestras, great museums, politicians, dropouts, traffic jams, a little air pollution—everything.

We are of this century, with all of the strengths and weaknesses and problems of people everywhere.

We will survive.

Because, above all, we are here. Alive. In a land called home.

The Airline of the People of Israel

The sabra generation were the iconic heroes of the Yishuv

For Ben-Gurion, an alliance with Britain was vital for the success of Zionism. However, in the early 1920s, as the Arabs became more militant and the British appeared to appease them (for example, by limiting Jewish immigration), **Vladimir Jabotinsky**, a Russian-born Jew, founded the **Revisionist Party** (its ideological successor today is the **Likud Party**). Though agreeing that British support was essential, Jabotinsky also believed that the Arabs would never willingly accept a Jewish state, and he called for the building of an "iron wall" of Jewish military force to counter the inevitable Arab resistance to the Jewish state. While Ben-Gurion and the Labor Zionists emphasised immigration and settlement as the route to statehood, Jabotinsky focused on military force as the key factor.

In the 1920s, the *Yishuv* grew stronger. Jewish land holdings doubled, and although they only represented a small portion of Palestine's cultivable land, they were concentrated in the more fertile coastal areas and inland valleys. Furthermore, although the Jews only constituted 20 percent of the population, the *Yishuv* and the idea of a Jewish homeland had the official support of the British Mandate, now enshrined in international law.

Personal Testimony
Jewish Settlers

Sixteen-year-old Joseph Baratz left Russia in 1906. He believed in social equality and sought to create a new way of life in Palestine. Later, he would go on to be one of the founders of the first kibbutz. However, when he visited the Jewish settlement of Rishon-le-Zion, soon after arriving in Palestine, he was surprised and disappointed by what he saw:

> It was a sad country, like a desert all the way until you came to the plantations of Rishon. Naturally we were excited when we saw them – in a moment we would see a Jewish village. But we thought that to talk with the Biluim [a particular group of Jewish immigrants] we would have to wait until sunset – we imagined a village like in Russia – hens pecking in the road, children shouting by the river, and not a soul in sight while the sun is high and all the peasants are in the fields.
>
> But what is this? We were in a pretty street of neat brick houses with red tiled roofs; from one of them came the tinkling of a piano. The street was full of people strolling up and down. We couldn't believe our eyes. We asked: "Who are these?"
>
> "Biluim."
>
> "And who does the work?"
>
> "The Arabs."
>
> "And what do the Jews do?"
>
> "They're managers, supervisors."

It was a great shock to us. I said to myself, "This isn't what I've come for," and I could see that the others were disappointed as well.[9]

Baratz expresses initial disillusionment, but a young woman known only as "R" (her name is not recorded) evidently embraced her life as a Zionist pioneer from the start. This extract is from her diary in 1925:

I have been here in Eretz Israel for eight months now, and it seems to have been a long period in my life. In the very first days after my arrival I already felt as if I had been born here. I have made it my goal to train myself for agricultural work as soon as I came here. This was the be-all and end-all for me. My only thought was of the proper way to get to a healthy economic position, to take roots in the soil. I was not yet sure that I could get used to physical work. But I strongly desired to take part in the process of creation and construction of a new settlement for my people. . . . In my work I found what I had been looking for. I work freely, without tension, and I find my work interesting. Here there is room for energy and initiative. This is the beginning of a self-sufficient farm, run by ourselves.

And, several years later, R wrote:

I am happy to be free, to have regained my energy and warmth, and to feel the firm ground under my feet. I believe in Eretz Israel and in the people. I am surrounded by people who have faith. My life is the life of the kibbutz in Israel.[10]

Arab Opposition to British Policy in Palestine

Many Palestinian Arabs opposed the Jewish "right of return" to their ancient homeland. They did not deny the discrimination and persecution that the Jews had experienced in Europe nor the Jews' historical and religious ties to the Holy Land. However, they rejected the idea that the Jews' humanitarian plight granted them special political and national rights in Palestine, and that those Jewish rights should take precedence over Arab rights. Below is an extract from the submission of the Palestine Arab Delegation to a British commission in the early 1920s:

> What confusion would ensue all the world over if this principle on which the Jews base their "legitimate" claim were carried out in other parts of the world! What migrations of nations must follow! The Spaniards in Spain would have to make room for the Arabs and Moors who conquered and ruled their country for over 700 years ..."

George Antonius, a Palestinian Christian, explains the basis of the Arab claim to Palestine:

> The Arab claims rest on two distinct foundations: the natural right of a settled population, in great majority agricultural, to remain in possession of the land of its birthright; and the acquired political rights which followed from the disappearance of Turkish sovereignty and from the Arab share in its overthrow, and which Great Britain is under contractual obligation to recognise and uphold.[12]

CHAPTER 3

British Rule in Palestine
1929–39

This chapter concerns the development of the conflict between Zionists and Arabs during the second decade of the British Mandate in Palestine. It will address the following questions:

- **What was the impact of British rule on the Arabs in Palestine?**
- **Did the riots of 1929 represent a turning point in the history of Palestine?**
- **How did Palestinian nationalism develop in the 1930s?**
- **What was the Arab Revolt and how did the British respond?**
- **What was the impact of the Revolt on Jews and Arabs in Palestine?**

The Impact of British Rule on the Arabs in Palestine

While the leadership of the *Yishuv* focused on developing the autonomous and representative institutions of a state in the making, the Arabs were effectively prevented from formulating any kind of representative body under the British Mandate in Palestine, although these were appearing in neighbouring Arab countries at that time.

Palestinian society, as introduced in chapter 1, was dominated by the "notables," traditional elites who, by and large, saw their own interests – their social and political standing – best served by cooperation with their new British rulers and continuing to act as intermediaries between the rulers and the ruled as they had in Ottoman times. Yet that cooperation meant accepting the Balfour Declaration's commitment to Zionism, now reinforced in the terms of the British Mandate. Furthermore, while the declaration recognised the Jews as a "people" with the right to a "national home," the Arabs were "communities" with only "civil and religious rights."

When the Arabs demanded their political rights, particularly the right to some form of representative government in what they saw as their own country, they were effectively told by the British that their rights were subordinate to those of the Jewish population of Palestine and that an Arab-dominated legislature or national council would not be allowed. In the words of the Palestinian historian Rashid Khalidi, the Arabs of Palestine felt that they were being kept in an "iron cage."[1]

In a show of religious solidarity, members of well-established and newer middle-class Palestinian families and religious leaders formed the Muslim-Christian Associations in the immediate postwar years. These bodies asserted a specifically Palestinian sense of national identity, declaring:

> Palestine is Arab. Its language is Arabic. We want to see this formally recognized. It was Great Britain that rescued us from Turkish tyranny and we do not believe that it will deliver us into the claws of the Jews. We ask for fairness and justice. We ask that it protect our rights and not decide the future of Palestine without asking our opinion.[2]

Like the notables, the Associations regularly petitioned the British rulers in the hope that they might abandon or, at least, moderate their support for Zionism and allow for a democratically elected parliament. They made little headway.

In 1921 the British, under Sir Herbert Samuel, made a move to win over the most prominent Palestinian family clan, the Husseinis. In 1921, they engineered the appointment of Haj Amin al-Husseini as Grand Mufti, the supreme Muslim authority in Palestine. Then, a year later, they set up the Supreme Muslim Council (see p. 28) for the same reason, but even more so as a gesture to demands for representative government. For the British, the policy of favouring one particular family had the added advantage that it might increase clan rivalry and division within the Palestinian leadership. Opposition to the Husseinis was led by another powerful Jerusalem family, the **Nashashibis**.

Arab grievances sometimes led to physical resistance, and there were occasional instances of peasants reoccupying land and attacking rural Jewish settlements, often in isolated, spontaneous acts of violence. On a larger scale, Arabs had attacked Jews in Jerusalem and Haifa in 1920 and 1921. However, it was the violence that erupted in Jerusalem in 1929 that was to have the greatest and most lasting impact on both the Jewish and the Arab communities.

The Riots of 1929: A Turning Point

The Arabs were increasingly alarmed by the growth in size and confidence of the *Yishuv*. By 1929, they could see how far the Zionists had come in developing their own separate economy and building the political foundations of a

The Dome of the Rock was built on the rock from which Muslims believe that Muhammad rose to heaven. Below it, in the foreground, is the Western or Wailing Wall, which Jews believe to be the last remaining part of the ancient Jewish Temple. (Photo by Peter Mullan)

separate state under a largely unified leadership. This had been achieved with the support of the British and funding from abroad. By contrast, the Arabs themselves lacked both unified leadership and representative institutions, as well as any foreign funding. Their political protest proved ineffective, and their leaders knew that to resort to physical forms of resistance would bring them into conflict with the British, the foremost power in the Middle East.

In 1928, a dispute arose over the control of and access to the Wailing Wall in Jerusalem. Jews believe this to be the last remaining part of the ancient Jewish temple of King Solomon and they have traditionally wept here over its destruction. The wall forms the western limit of what Muslims call Haram al-Sharif and Jews call Temple Mount. The gold-topped Dome of the Rock and the al-Aqsa Mosque were built on the rock from which, Muslims believe, the Prophet Muhammad ascended to heaven.

Rumors of a Zionist plot to take control of the Muslim holy places were widely believed among the Arabs and led to outbreaks of violence that continued into 1929. Then, in August 1929, demonstrations by extreme Zionists, inspired by Jabotinsky (see p. 32) and the publication of leaflets calling on Arabs in nearby villages to come to Jerusalem and "save" the holy sites, led to an escalation in the violence. Several Jews were killed in Jerusalem and the violence spilled over into surrounding areas with attacks on Jewish kibbutzim.

The worst violence of all took place in the town of Hebron (see map on p. 41), south of Jerusalem. This was home to the Tomb of the Patriarchs, which is holy to both Muslims and Jews.[3] When Muslims in Hebron heard reports of Arabs killed in Jerusalem and threats to their holy sites, they attacked the Jewish quarter. In a town where Jews had lived peacefully for hundreds of years, sixty-four of them were killed. Other Jews in Hebron were saved by their Arab neighbours who hid them in their own homes, putting themselves in danger. Altogether, 113 Jews and 116 Arabs were killed in Jerusalem, Hebron, and other places. Most of the Arabs were killed by British troops after reinforcements were brought in.

The Jews killed in Hebron and several of those killed in Jerusalem were members of the Old *Yishuv*, often highly religious Sephardi Jews who did not support Zionism. In the eyes of their attackers, that made no difference and they either did not know or did not care to make the distinction. After the killings, the remaining Jews left Hebron and many Jewish merchants abandoned their businesses in the largely Arab Old City of Jerusalem and moved to majority-Jewish neighbourhoods.

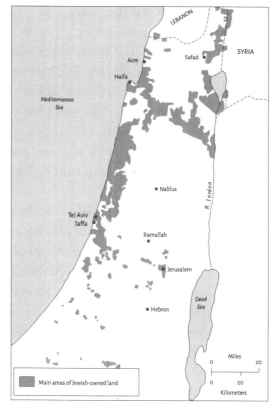

The main areas of Jewish settlement in Palestine in the 1920s

Across Palestine the events of 1929 led to increased physical separation between Jewish and Arab communities. After 1929, Jews who had not been Zionists increasingly looked to the Zionist leadership in Palestine for protection. Increased separation strengthened support for Zionist ideology and leadership and made for a more unified Jewish community.

The whole *Yishuv* was shocked by the intensity of the hatred displayed in the violence of 1929 and the inability of the British forces to halt the killings. The Jewish community had seen that the British had lost control in Jerusalem despite all the warning signs of simmering unrest since 1928. Many of the Arabs serving in the British police refused to carry out orders to fire on fellow Arabs. The events of 1929 revealed to Ben-Gurion how vulnerable the *Yishuv* was. In public, he blamed the violence on those who were "incited and inflamed by the fire of religion and fanaticism," but privately he acknowledged the reality of a confrontation between two national communities that both aspired to an independent state in Palestine.[4]

In some parts of Palestine, life continued as if the violence and deaths had not occurred. Many of the growing number of citrus plantations, both Jewish- and Arab-owned, continued to employ mixed labour forces, and Arabs and Jews worked together in the British administration. However, the Zionist leadership intensified the campaign for exclusively Jewish labour on Jewish-owned farms and in Jewish-owned industries. Above all, the conquest of land became the overriding priority: over half the budget of the Jewish Agency was spent on the purchase of land in the 1930s. New Jewish settlements were built in more easily defendable positions, while the Haganah was reorganised and a new, more aggressive military body, the **Irgun**, was formed by Jabotinsky's Revisionists in 1931.

The British government conducted an inquiry into the riots. While aware of the religious issue that sparked the attacks, it recognised that "a landless and discontented class is being created" by Jewish land purchases and the increasing use of Jewish-only labour on Jewish-owned lands. The Passfield White Paper, a special report making recommendations to the government, proposed to restrict both immigration and land sales. It aroused fury within the WZO in London, and Weizmann and his Zionist colleagues, backed by many in the opposition Conservative Party, exerted sufficient pressure to have it reversed by the Labour government. In effect, the British government reaffirmed its commitment to the development of the Jewish National Home. For the Arabs, this was further betrayal by the British.

The Development of Palestinian Nationalism in the 1930s

The events of 1929 did not only act as a stimulus to the development of the *Yishuv*; they also had a major impact on the development of Palestinian nationalism. The leadership of the Palestinian notables, especially of the Jerusalem-based Husseinis, was increasingly criticised in the 1930s. The Grand Mufti, Haj Amin al-Husseini, and his allies continued to work with the British, relying on diplomacy and international support to end, or at least modify, the Balfour Declaration.

Yet this policy of collaboration with the British showed no sign of leading to any reduction in Zionist immigration and settlement on the land. The traditional leadership was increasingly challenged by a younger generation of urban-educated Palestinians, and a more assertive popular movement emerged. The Young Men's Muslim Association (YMMA), modeled on the British Young Men's Christian Association (YMCA), was one example of a newer, more distinctly nationalist organisation. Many of its members were journalists, teachers, and other professionals.

Anti-British and anti-Zionist agitation became more and more militant, with some calling for armed resistance. On occasion, the British responded with force. In October 1933, a large Arab demonstration was violently dispersed in Jerusalem, and two weeks later, twenty-six Arabs were killed by British police during a demonstration in Jaffa. Ben-Gurion, the Zionist leader, noted that the demonstrators had been highly disciplined and acknowledged that they would be admired as "national heroes" in their own community. He was in no doubt about the strength of Palestinian national feeling.

Another factor in the strengthening of the Palestinian national movement was the rate of Jewish immigration, which began to soar after 1933 when Adolf Hitler came to power in Germany and Nazi anti-Semitism drove many Jews abroad. The number of immigrants to Palestine increased from ten thousand in 1932 to sixty-two thousand in 1935, and the *Yishuv* doubled in size in the same time period. This surge in numbers increased the demand for the land that agents of the JNF bought for the establishment of new settlements. While a growing number of smaller Arab landowners benefited from selling their land, a far larger number of families were displaced from farms they had cultivated as tenant farmers.

Year	Number of Jews	Number of Arabs
1919	65,000	700,000
1929	160,000	1 million
1939	430,000	1.2 million
1947	600,000	1.3 million

Jewish and Arab populations in Palestine, 1919–47

The dispossession and displacement of peasant families were not the only reasons for increasing discontent among the rural population. With the growth of the urban population, both Arab and Jewish, the demand for food increased. The larger landowners could afford to invest in large-scale, commercial agriculture to satisfy the demand, but many smaller ones could not afford to do so, or they borrowed from Arab moneylenders and became engulfed in debt. Many farmers were hit further by the collapse in prices for agricultural goods resulting from the worldwide depression after the Wall Street Crash of 1929.

By 1936, a third of all rural Palestinian males were forced to find work outside the villages, either because of land sales or indebtedness. This partly explains why peasants provided so much support for the Arab Revolt of 1936.

al-Qassam and Armed Resistance

An increasing number of landless peasants made their way to cities like Haifa and Jaffa. These coastal towns had benefited from British investment in railways and other communications and, in the case of Haifa, from the building of an oil refinery and port, through which passed the oil from British-owned fields in Iraq. However,

Izz ad-Din al-Qassam

not all prospered because of this growth and thousands of dispossessed peasants and casual workers lived in poverty in the cities. Many of them found a champion in **Izz ad-Din al-Qassam**.

Born in Syria, al-Qassam had been forced to flee from his homeland after fighting against French occupation at the end of the First World War. An impassioned orator, he became a teacher and preacher to those on the margins of society in Haifa. He called for armed struggle against colonial rule and Zionist settlement, made more urgent, in his view, by the discovery of arms being smuggled into Palestine by Jews in October 1935. This suggested that the Zionists were preparing for armed confrontation.

In November 1935, al-Qassam took to the hills with a small band of followers to launch a guerrilla war. As it turned out, he was hunted down and killed by the British. His fight was short-lived, but his actions galvanised peasants and townsmen and he became a hero to the Palestinian cause. Thousands attended his funeral in a huge demonstration of national unity.

The Arab Revolt, 1936–39

Fighting broke out between Arabs and Jews in Tel Aviv and Jaffa in April 1936. There was rioting and killing, and curfews were imposed. Calls were issued for Arab workers and government employees to embark on a general strike.

So began what Arabs called the "Great Rebellion." It was led by young Palestinians, but it embraced merchants and shopkeepers, town workers, and Arabs who worked in Jewish settlements. So-called national committees emerged, first in Nablus, then in other towns, to coordinate the strike, enforce a boycott of British and Jewish goods, and raise money to compensate strikers for their loss of earnings.

The older Palestinian leaders were hesitant, with Haj Amin al-Husseini calling for restraint in any confrontations with the British. But the traditional leaders capitulated, as they understood the desperation of many peasants and townsfolk and did not wish to lose control of events. The different factions among the notables temporarily sank their differences and formed the **Arab Higher Committee (AHC)**.

Haj Amin al-Husseini became leader and assumed overall direction of the general strike and responsibility for dealing with the British.

The AHC demanded a democratically elected legislature and an end to Jewish immigration and land sales. They hoped that widespread resistance would force a policy change within what they saw as the pro-Zionist British administration.

In Haifa and Jaffa, Palestinians shot at British police stations and bombed Jewish targets. For several days, they took control of Jaffa. The British responded by destroying much of the old center, justifying their actions as necessary for "urban improvement." Strikes and boycotts were accompanied by marches and meetings.

Widespread fighting broke out in the countryside. It started gradually, with isolated incidents: Arab farmers fought to prevent being evicted from land bought by Jews, and villagers attacked Jews cultivating traditional village land which had been sold to them. But then, Arab bands cut telephone lines and attacked isolated British police stations and Jewish settlements. By September 1936, two hundred Arabs, eighty Jews, and twenty-eight British had been killed.

The strike was largely unsuccessful. Arab workers in Jewish businesses who went on strike were simply replaced by Jewish workers, while Arab employees of the British government lost their ability to influence government policies if they went on strike. The strike in the Arab port of Haifa resulted in the more rapid development of the largely Jewish port of Tel Aviv. The strike served to strengthen the growth of a separate, stronger Jewish economy. Ben-Gurion knew that economic independence was an important step toward political independence.

Meanwhile, the AHC acknowledged the damage done to Arab business, especially the cultivation and export of citrus fruit. By July 1936, the urban revolt was subsiding. After the British proposed to set up a commission of inquiry, the strike was called off in October 1936. Meanwhile, twenty thousand extra British troops were brought in to regain control of the towns. However, much of the countryside was in open revolt: Palestine was caught up in a civil war that was to last for three years and cost thousands more lives.

The Peel Partition Plan, 1937

Led by Lord Peel, members of the Commission of Inquiry interviewed over one hundred people in Palestine – British, Jewish, and Arab. The Zionists demanded unlimited immigration and land sales, while Amin al-Husseini went further than he had done before by calling for an Arab state of Palestine and the expulsion of all the Jews who had immigrated since the First World War. The report of the Peel Commission, published in July 1937, concluded that cooperation between Arabs and Jews was impossible:

> An irrepressible conflict has arisen between two national communities within the narrow bounds of one small country. There is no common ground between them. Their national aspirations are incompatible.[5]

In other words, the report recognised that the League of Nations Mandate was unworkable. It recommended the partition of Palestine into two separate states, one Jewish and the other Arab. The proposed Jewish state would consist of about 20 percent of Palestine, including much of the most fertile land on the coast and inland valleys where many Jews had settled. The Jewish Agency agreed to the partition plan, although its leaders wanted more land than they were allocated.

But even then, many Jews in Palestine foresaw that they would have to fight to defend a Jewish state. In a speech to members of the Jewish Agency in May 1936, Ben-Gurion had concluded that only war, not negotiation, would resolve the conflict. He did not use the term "iron wall" but he recognised that only force would enable the Jews to establish an independent state in Palestine.

Ben-Gurion was one of several Jewish leaders who wanted Palestine in its entirety to be made into a Jewish state. He accepted Peel's Partition Plan because he knew that the Jews were not yet strong enough to demand more. Therefore, the official policy of the Jewish Agency was to accept a Jewish state in part of Palestine, alongside an Arab one. Ben-Gurion assumed that an independent state, however small, would allow for unlimited Jewish immigration, the development of a strong economy, and the organisation of a powerful army. Then, after that, as he said in a letter to his son in October 1937, Jews would be able to settle in all parts of Palestine:

> I am certain we will be able to settle in all the other parts of the country, whether through agreement and mutual understanding with our Arab neighbours or in another way.[6]

As well as recommending partition, the Peel Commission accepted the concept of population transfer: that over two hundred thousand Arabs should be transferred out of the proposed Jewish state into the Arab one and 1,250 Jews transferred the other way. The aim was to ensure that Jews were not outnumbered by Arabs in the Jewish state. The idea of population transfer had been a consistent feature of Zionist thinking since Herzl, and especially after 1929. The Arabs could join their kinsfolk in neighbouring Arab countries, so it was argued. All they had to do was "to fold their tents and silently steal away," as Israel Zangwill had declared in 1905.[7]

With Peel's recommendation, the idea of transfer could be seen to have gained legitimacy, although it remained highly sensitive. In 1938, the British dropped the recommendation of population transfer but its very public airing by the mandatory power made the prospect of transfer of the Arab population more feasible.

A small minority of Zionists opposed the partition plan, believing in the possibility of a "bi-national state" in which the two nations, the Jews and the Arabs, could live on the same land. Arab opposition to the plan was immediate: the AHC and most of the Arab population rejected partition. They feared exactly what Ben-Gurion envisaged: that a small Jewish state would provide the base from which to launch further expansion. The fighting now entered a more violent stage.

The Revolt in the Countryside

In September 1937, the AHC was banned by the British after the killing of an official, and al-Husseini escaped into exile in Lebanon.[8] The leadership of the revolt was now taken up by local commanders, mostly peasants. It was largely fueled by rural despair and hatred of the big landowners, some of whom were suspected of having sold land secretly to the Jews.

Arab fighters, 1938. This photograph was found on the body of an Arab rebel leader who was killed by British troops.

By October 1937, armed bands were roaming the countryside, often inspired by the example of Izz ad-Din al-Qassam. They carried out attacks on British forces, cut telephone lines, destroyed bridges, and attacked Jewish settlements. They also destroyed parts of the oil pipeline from Iraq to Haifa.

There were estimated to be about ten thousand fighters, even if only three thousand were full-time, and they included some non-Palestinian Arabs from Syria and Iraq. These forces largely controlled the central highlands of Palestine until the end of 1938. They collected taxes, established their own courts, and dealt with informers and collaborators. They killed several Arab leaders who were accused of collaboration with the British, as well as Arabs serving in the British Police. A number of killings were the result of internal political feuds, while many members of the so-called peace bands, organised by the Nashashibi clan to fight alongside the British, were killed.

The British responded ruthlessly. They hanged over a hundred Arabs and carried out targeted assassinations and deportations. They made use of mass arrests and held thousands without trial. They destroyed houses suspected of containing Arab terrorists or arms and they imposed harsh collective punishments on whole villages. All these tactics would later be adopted by the Haganah and, after 1948, by the **Israel Defense Forces (IDF)**.

The British also helped to train and organise the Haganah and set up special Jewish "night squads" to hunt down rebels under cover of darkness. The Revisionist splinter group, Irgun, adopted terrorist tactics and, in late 1937, placed bombs in marketplaces, killing seventy-seven Arabs.

The fighting between Arabs, Jews, and British forces lasted for three years, from 1936 to 1939. Eventually, with the help of more troops, air power, better weapons, and transport, the British were able to regain control of Palestine.

The Results of the Great Revolt

The very survival of the *Yishuv*, the Jewish community in Palestine, was undoubtedly under threat during the years from 1936 to 1939. It is unlikely that it could have withstood the Arab Revolt without the support of overwhelming British military force. Britain had provided the "iron wall" necessary for the survival of the Zionist project. Not a single Jewish settlement was destroyed, while thirty new ones were established.

Jewish immigration continued, and by 1939, Jews made up 30 percent of the population of Palestine. Under the protection of the British, the economic and military development of the *Yishuv* accelerated. It was far stronger, better organised, and more secure by 1939 than it had been before the Revolt. Many Jews abandoned mixed neighbourhoods in cities like Haifa and Jaffa, while the city of Tel Aviv continued its development as a modern port and industrial center. Its population grew to 165,000. Most crucial of all, about 15,000 Jews gained military training, experience, and funding from the British, which would be highly significant in the confrontation that was to take place with Arab forces in 1948–49.

On the Arab side, the Revolt led to the emergence of a mass movement that had great importance, even if it was primarily symbolic, for the development of Palestinian nationalism. The example of al-Qassam, although he was killed before the Revolt started, was to be a source of inspiration for the **Palestine Liberation Organization (PLO)** of the 1960s and 1970s and for thousands of Palestinians during the First **Intifada** of the late 1980s. However, the loosely organised, locally based resistance that enabled the rebels to control large swaths of Palestine from late 1937 to the end of 1938 could not, ultimately, hide the fact that the leadership was divided and there was no central command or control of the rebellion. Many of the traditional leaders, the urban notables, were distrusted and thousands of wealthier Palestinians had fled to neighbouring states. About 10 percent of the Arab male population was killed, wounded, or deported and large numbers of weapons and ammunition were seized by the British. As the historian Rashid Khalidi wrote:

> These heavy military losses were to affect the Palestinians profoundly a few years later when Britain handed the Palestine question over to the United Nations, and it became clear that an open battle for control of the country between Arabs and Jews would take place.[9]

Both the elimination of much of the actual and potential Arab leadership and the British contribution to the development of the *Yishuv*'s military forces were to be of huge significance in the civil war that developed after the publication of the UN's Partition Plan in November 1947.

For the time being, Ben-Gurion realised that a continuing alliance with Britain was indispensable for the success of Zionism. Although he acknowledged, after the outbreak of the Arab Revolt, that a military confrontation with the Arabs was unavoidable at some stage, he believed that continued cooperation with the British was necessary.

The British Government White Paper, 1939

By 1939, when the rebellion ended, the British government had given up all further ideas of partition. The Palestine Mandate was increasingly seen as a costly burden that was alienating Arab populations in the region. As the prospect of another world war increased, Britain feared the growth of friendship between Arab leaders and Germany. Britain needed to keep neighbouring Arab countries on their side so that oil supplies from the Middle East would continue to reach Britain.

The government issued a white paper declaring that Britain wanted an independent Palestine within ten years. This would be neither a Jewish nor Arab state but one in which Arabs and Jews shared governing responsibility. Meanwhile, Britain would continue to rule Palestine. The White Paper also said that Britain would restrict Jewish immigration:

For each of the next five years a quota of 10,000 Jewish immigrants will be allowed.

In addition, as a contribution towards the solution of the Jewish refugee problem, 25,000 refugees will be admitted.

After the period of five years no further Jewish immigration will be permitted unless the Arabs of Palestine are prepared to acquiesce in it.[10]

Not surprisingly, the Jewish population was furious. On the outbreak of war in September 1939, Ben-Gurion said that the Jews would necessarily side with Britain against Nazi Germany but "the Jews would fight with the British as though there was no white paper, and would fight against the white paper as if there was no war."[11]

Personal Testimony
Arab Resistance

Two of the extracts below focus on the violence that erupted in Jerusalem, Hebron, and other towns in 1929. The first comes from London's *Daily Mail*, reporting Jewish eyewitness accounts of what happened in Hebron:

Chief Rabbi Slonim . . . said: "A band of Arabs broke into the Talmudic College, killing one student. Other students escaped to the cellars of a neighboring house. Taking our lives in our hands, I and my friends went to see the chief of police. He refused to see us. On Saturday morning, the Arabs broke into our house. A friendly Arab stood in front of me to protect me and swore he would be killed himself rather than that I should be harmed."

A student said: "Those in the house of the rabbi's son barred their doors, took hold of Bibles and holy books and recited psalms and hymns. Yelling, the Arabs smashed their way into the house with axes and iron bars. Eighteen of those in the house were killed ... The Arab police stood by while the massacre continued. Then the Arabs began looting and the reign of terror lasted until next day when armed British police arrived. They ended the rioting by shooting thirty of the Arabs on the spot."[12]

This second extract is from an article in an Arab newspaper, four years later. The author views the actions taken by the Arabs in a decidedly heroic light:

Today is the anniversary of the August uprising [of 1929] . . . the flames of which were borne high on this day in 1929. That day was a day of brilliance and glory in the annals of Palestinian-Arab history. This is the day of honour, splendour and sacrifice.

We attacked Western conquest and the Mandate and the Zionists upon our land. The Jews have coveted our endowments and yearned to take over our holy places. In our silence, they had seen a sign of weakness, therefore there was no more room in our hearts for patience or peace; no sooner had the Jews begun marching along this shameful road than the Arabs stood up, checked the oppression, and sacrificed their pure and noble souls on the sacred altar of nationalism.[13]

The last piece comes from a letter written by a young British official in Palestine. Here, he gives his view of the Arab general strike of 1936:

For the present, it seems as if the killing of Jews by Arabs and of Arabs by police has left off, which is a comfort, and the unrest has taken the form of what looks like it may become a prolonged general strike among Arabs. That is a better way of putting pressure on the government, I think, though it is bound to involve a lot of suffering for the workers and shopkeepers who strike. At present the strike is not complete. Most of the Arab shops all over the country are shut, except food shops, restaurants and cafes. The port is working here [in Tel Aviv] but at Jaffa I think work has stopped. The railways are still working, but there isn't much road communication between the large towns – Jewish cars and lorries move mostly under convoy.[14]

CHAPTER 4

UN Partition, Israel, and War
1945–49

In 1948 the British left Palestine, and the State of Israel was established. Israeli and Palestinian narratives differ markedly, particularly on the exodus of Palestinian Arabs and Israel's victory in the war that followed.

- **Why did the British decide to withdraw from Palestine?**
- **Why did the UN Partition Plan lead to civil war?**
- **What caused the exodus of Palestinian Arabs?**
- **How and why did Israel win the war of 1948–49?**

The End of the British Mandate

Palestine was relatively quiet during the Second World War. The Arabs were exhausted and leaderless at the end of the Revolt, while the establishment of a huge British military base and the consequent demand for food and other locally produced goods ushered in a period of economic prosperity.

The Zionists had suffered a setback in the form of the 1939 White Paper, in which the British dropped the idea of a Jewish state. However, most Jews in Palestine decided to support Britain in the fight against Nazi Germany. Some fought in the British Army, which enabled them to gain valuable military experience and even weapons. In 1944, Jewish volunteers from Palestine were organised into a specifically Jewish Brigade in the British Army.

The British were preoccupied with winning the war against Germany and they gave little thought to the future of Palestine. They maintained their policy of controlling Jewish immigration so as not to antagonise the Arabs, but this simply increased Zionist fears that the British would abandon the promises they had made to support a Jewish homeland.

Ben-Gurion and the Zionist leadership came to realise that the foreign power whose support they should seek was the emerging superpower of the United States. In May 1942, this became clearer after those attending a Zionist conference in the US declared their support for a "Jewish commonwealth" in all of Palestine. This became known as the Biltmore Program, after the name of the hotel in New York – the city with the largest Jewish population in the world, then and now – in which the conference was held. Now Ben-Gurion spoke of the "ruthless compulsion" needed to bring about the transfer of Arabs, so that only a "manageable" number of them were left in the Jewish state.

When the war ended in 1945, the British announced that there would be no change in their policy in Palestine. In other words, there would be no big increase in immigration and no separate Jewish state. But the war had toughened the resolve of the Zionists: six million Jews had been killed in the Nazi Holocaust and the Zionists were not in the mood to be patient. They were convinced that they had justice on their side and that international public opinion was coming round to support the idea of an independent Jewish state.

In August 1945, the Zionist Conference in London abandoned the gradualist policy of continuing to negotiate with the British, which Weizmann and the London-based WZO had favoured, and demanded the immediate creation of a

Jewish state and a policy of active opposition to British rule in Palestine. Jewish leaders in Palestine ordered the Haganah, the Jewish paramilitary organisation, to cooperate with Irgun and the **Stern Gang**, a breakaway group of militant Zionists. British military bases, railways, trains, and bridges in Palestine, as well as the oil pipeline to Haifa, became the targets of these groups.

On the diplomatic front, the Zionists decided that only the United States could put enough pressure on Britain to agree to a separate Jewish state and leave Palestine. The Zionists had the support of much of the Jewish population in the US, who in turn put pressure on the US government. There were 4.5 million Jewish Americans, 2 million of them in New York City alone. By the end of the war, a majority were Zionists, convinced of the need to establish an independent Jewish state for the Jewish refugees who had survived the Nazi Holocaust in Europe.

After the war, American Zionists, often joined by Jewish leaders from Palestine, launched a propaganda offensive: they addressed meetings, held rallies, placed advertisements, and, above all, lobbied members of the US government and Congress. In April 1946, the US president, Harry Truman, called on the British government to allow the immediate entry of a hundred thousand Jewish refugees to Palestine. Six months later, he came out in support of the partition of Palestine.

The Palestinian Arabs continued to oppose the idea of a Jewish state in Palestine, which they feared would be filled by immigrants from Europe who would demand further expansion and a Jewish state incorporating all of Palestine. Besides, many Arabs argued that the West should take responsibility for the victims of the Holocaust and it was unfair to see Palestine as the solution to a European problem. The West may have seen the Jewish question as one of settling refugees, but for the Palestinians, it was one of being displaced by incoming settlers. They demanded an end to Jewish immigration and the declaration of an independent Palestinian state.

Meanwhile, the British authorities stopped boatloads of illegal Jewish immigrants from landing in Palestine. They knew that Jewish immigration angered the Arabs and, when violence broke out between Jews and Arabs, British troops and police had to keep order. The British refused to agree to any increase in immigration as they realised that further Jewish immigration would be resisted by the Arabs and could lead to civil war. The Haganah, for their part, did all they could to obstruct the British and to assist immigration.

Jewish Terrorism

Jewish attacks on British forces increased, sometimes in retaliation for death sentences passed on Jewish fighters. In July 1946, Irgun carried out their most spectacular act of terrorism – an attack on the King David Hotel in Jerusalem, which housed the British military headquarters in Palestine. It was protected by barbed wire, machine guns, and soldiers on patrol.

The King David Hotel was blown up by Irgun forces in July 1946.

61

At noon on July 22, 1946, a truck drove up to the entrance of the hotel kitchen. Men dressed as Arabs got out and unloaded their cargo of milk churns. They rolled them into the building. No one guessed that the milk churns contained high explosives or that the men were members of Irgun. At 12:37 PM the explosion tore through the building, killing ninety-one people, including fifteen Jews.

Terrorist incidents like these weakened the morale of the British, both in Palestine and at home. They also led to frustration and anger at what Britain saw as support for terrorism from American Zionists. After the killing of twenty British soldiers in the officers' club in Jerusalem in February 1947, Clement Attlee, the British prime minister, complained of a report he had heard that the mayor of New York had launched a Zionist drive to raise £2 million for the purchase of "men, guns and money." Atlee protested that "the guns which are being subscribed for in America can only be required to shoot at British soldiers in Palestine."[1]

This photograph appeared on the front page of the British newspaper the *Daily Express* in August 1947. It shows two British soldiers who were hanged by members of Irgun as revenge for the execution of three of Irgun's members.

The *Theodore Herzl* refugee ship arrived in Palestine with 25,000 refugees on board. The banner on the ship reads, "The Germans destroyed our families and homes – don't you destroy our hopes."

Two incidents in the summer of 1947 finally convinced the British to withdraw from Palestine. One was the killing of two British soldiers in revenge for the execution of three Irgun members. A photograph of the two men hanging from a tree appeared on the front page of several British newspapers.

The other incident involved the *Exodus*, a ship that was carrying 4,500 refugees from Europe. It was prevented by the British authorities from landing its passengers in Palestine and was sent back to Europe. This incident attracted widespread publicity, winning much sympathy for the Jewish refugees, and was a huge public relations success for the Zionists as the British authorities came under worldwide criticism.

Furthermore, the British were exhausted after the Second World War, with food shortages and rationing at home, and could hardly afford to keep a hundred thousand troops and police in Palestine. After thirty years of ruling Palestine, the British government decided that it would hand over its responsibility to the United Nations.

The UN Partition Plan and Civil War, 1947–48

As early as February 1947, the British government sought the advice of the United Nations, which had been formed at the end of the Second World War. The UN Special Committee on Palestine (UNSCOP) was set up to investigate and make recommendations on how to resolve the Palestine problem. The UNSCOP report was completed in August.

In November, the UN General Assembly voted to accept the recommendations of the UNSCOP report by thirty-three votes to thirteen (with ten abstentions). The main recommendation was to divide Palestine and set up both a Jewish and an Arab state. The areas that were more Jewish (in population and land ownership) were to be allocated to the Jewish state and those that were mainly Arab to the Arab state.

Although the Jews made up one-third of the population and owned less than 10 percent of the land, they were to be given 55 percent of the overall territory, including the sparsely populated Negev Desert. Increased territory was allotted to the Jewish state partly so that it could accommodate Jewish refugees stranded in Europe.

In what was to be the Jewish state, there was an existing Jewish population of 520,000 and an Arab population of 400,000. The suggested partition presented a crisscross arrangement with "kissing points" at the intersections. The UN thought, rather optimistically, that this would force the two sides to cooperate. An international zone governed by an international force was to encompass the holy cities of Jerusalem and Bethlehem.

The reorganised AHC, representing the Palestinian Arabs, rejected the UN Partition Plan, especially as the designated Jewish state was larger and contained some cities, such as

Haifa, with Arab majorities. The Jewish Agency in Palestine accepted the plan: the Jews in Palestine were pleased that they now had international support for the idea of a Jewish state.

However, not all Jews in Palestine were happy with the plan. Jerusalem, with its Jewish-majority population, was excluded from the Jewish state, and many Jewish settlements were to be included in the Arab state. David Ben-Gurion said, "Tens of thousands of our youth are prepared to lay down their lives for the sake of Jerusalem. It is within the boundaries of the State of Israel just as Tel Aviv is."[2]

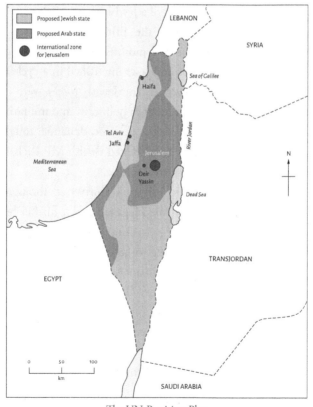

The UN Partition Plan

Menachem Begin, leader of Irgun (and a future prime minister of Israel), announced, "The partition of the homeland is illegal. It will never be recognised. It will not bind the Jewish people. Jerusalem was and will forever be our capital. *Eretz* Israel will be restored to the people of Israel. All of it. And forever."[3]

Civil War in Palestine, November 1947–May 1948

A few days after the UN voted for partition, the AHC proclaimed a three-day strike, leading to outbreaks of violence against Jewish civilians. The Jewish Agency and its forces were ready to respond. They had always known that the Arabs would resist the establishment of a Jewish state in Palestine.

In December 1947, when the British announced that they would leave Palestine five months later in May 1948, the fighting between Arabs and Jews intensified in a cycle of attack, retaliation, and revenge. The Jewish forces were far better prepared than the Arabs, both politically and militarily. The Jewish Agency was "the most efficient, dynamic, toughest organisation I have ever seen," noted British MP Richard Crossman on an official visit to Palestine.[4]

The Agency had at its disposal thirty-five thousand trained men and women in the Haganah and a further few thousand in Irgun and the Stern Gang. At first, the Jewish forces acted defensively, seeking to hold on to the land they had been allocated. The Palestinian Arabs, by contrast, had a deeply divided leadership, very limited finances, and no single national authority to raise, organise, and lead a military force. In 1948, volunteers from Syria and Iraq began to cross into Palestine to help. They were sponsored by the recently formed **Arab League** and were formed into the Arab Liberation Army (ALA).

This was no surprise to the Jewish leaders. They fully expected neighbouring Arab states to invade Palestine when the British left and the new Jewish state came into existence. In March, the Haganah commanders came up with Plan Dalet (Plan D), the two main aims of which were to:

- take over any installations evacuated by the British, especially military bases
- carry out the "destruction and expulsion or occupation" of Arab villages in the future Jewish state.

Already, by February 1948, many of the Palestinian elite, such as landowners and businessmen, had left Palestine to escape the fighting. This contributed to insecurity among the Arab masses, especially in villages, and encouraged others to leave.

Then, in April 1948, Jewish forces began the forcible expulsion of Arabs from villages inside what was to become the Jewish state. Nearly all the villages along the coast from Tel Aviv to Haifa were cleared of their Arab populations.

The Israeli historian Ilan Pappe explains how Jewish forces "surrounded each village on three sides and put the villagers to flight through the fourth side."[5] If people refused to leave, they were often forced onto trucks and driven to Transjordan. Jewish forces also took over mixed Arab-Jewish towns, such as in Haifa where explosions were set off in Arab areas of the city. Nearly all of the Arab population of seventy thousand fled the city.

In the weeks before the British withdrawal from Palestine, some of the bloodiest fighting took place in and around Jerusalem, where a hundred thousand Jews were running short of food. Massacres of civilians were carried out by both sides.

Some of the attacks by Jewish forces were in retaliation for Arab attacks on Jewish settlements or on convoys trying to supply Jerusalem's Jewish population.

A widely publicised incident took place in April 1948 in the village of Deir Yassin. It was the last village on the western side of Jerusalem whose Arab inhabitants had not fled. On April 9, Irgun fighters, led by Menachem Begin, attacked the village and killed over a hundred inhabitants, seventy-five of whom were elderly, women, or children. Begin himself later wrote of the effects:

> Throughout the Arab world and the world at large, a wave of lying propaganda was let loose about "Jewish atrocities" . . . The Arabs began to flee in terror, even before they clashed with Jewish forces . . . Arab propaganda spread a legend of terror amongst Arabs and Arab troops, who were seized with panic at the mention of Irgun soldiers. The legend was worth half a dozen battalions to the forces of Israel.[6]

The Arabs took revenge a few days later when they ambushed a convoy on its way to a hospital in Jerusalem and killed seventy-eight people, including doctors and nurses.

Contrasting Narratives of the Palestinian Exodus

By the time the British left on May 14, 1948, over three hundred thousand Arabs had fled from what was to be the independent State of Israel. Ever since, there has been continuing debate over whether the Palestinians were expelled or chose to leave.

Palestinian refugees, carrying whatever possessions they can, make their way to safety during the fighting in 1948.

The Zionist Interpretation: The Arabs Left Voluntarily

The conventional Zionist interpretation is that Jewish military actions after November 1947 were largely defensive. They were designed to protect Jewish settlements and the roads linking them, especially the more isolated settlements like those in the Negev Desert. Jewish forces were also determined to keep open the roads to Jerusalem, where there were about 2,500 Jews living in the Old City who were regularly besieged. Some of the most intense fighting took place on these roads and in nearby villages.

In the case of coastal towns like Haifa and Jaffa, so the standard Zionist history goes, thousands of Arabs followed the example of their leaders, both civilian and military, and fled. Furthermore, their leaders called on them, in the press and on the radio, to leave, assuring them that they would be able to return with conquering Arab armies and reclaim their property and their livelihoods.

Alternative explanations for the Arab exodus have been offered ever since. A few of them have come from Israeli historians. However, the Israeli historians who challenged the standard interpretation laid themselves open to accusations of being unpatriotic, betraying those who gave their lives for their country and who ensured that the State of Israel was able to defend itself and survive once those Arab armies did invade. The standard Zionist interpretation remained predominant, both in Israel itself and in the West, for many years.

The Revisionist Interpretation: The Arabs Were Expelled
From the 1980s, more critical explanations for the Arab exodus were published, both in Israel itself and beyond. The emergence of these revisionist interpretations is partly explained by the release of official Israeli government documents. Like the British, the Israelis had adopted a rule whereby many secret papers could be declassified and opened to scrutiny by historians after thirty years. Thus, documents dealing with the last years of British rule became available starting in the late 1970s.

These interpretations, such as those written by the Israeli historians Benny Morris[7] and Ilan Pappe,[8] challenged the conventional interpretation. They pointed out that the Haganah and the Jewish Agency condoned, or certainly turned a blind eye to, some of the operations carried out by Irgun and the Stern Gang. The Jewish Agency *did* reprimand the perpetrators of the Deir Yassin Massacre, but, as Menachem Begin admitted, the effect of the massacre was to make tens of thousands more Palestinians flee from surrounding Arab villages in the few weeks between the massacre and the proclamation of the State of Israel.

The newer, more critical histories also interpreted what happened in large coastal towns such as Haifa and Jaffa rather differently. They pointed out that Jewish armed forces were determined to persuade as many Arabs to leave as possible to ensure that the forthcoming Israeli state was predominantly Jewish. Jewish loudspeakers broadcast into the Arab quarters news of what had happened in Deir Yassin. The forces of Irgun and the Stern Gang threw bombs into crowded Arab streets and aided the Haganah forces in their campaign to expel as many Arabs as possible. Despite claims by many historians, there is no recorded evidence of Arab leaders calling on their people, by loudspeaker or radio, to flee quickly from their homes.

The Haganah's Plan D may not have been a precise blueprint for the mass expulsion of Palestinian Arabs. It was general, even vague in parts, as Ilan Pappe has written. However:

> No less important than the plan was the atmosphere created, which paved the way for the ethnic cleansing operation in Palestine. Thus, while the actions of the *Haganah* had no clear and specific local directives, [the plan] was executed because the soldiers in the battlefield were oriented by a general attitude from above and motivated by remarks made by the *Yishuv*'s leaders on the need to "clean" the country. These remarks were translated into acts of depopulation by enthusiastic commanders on the ground, who knew that their actions would be justified in retrospect by the political leadership.[9]

Conclusion

Broad agreement among historians has emerged in recent years. The works of the "New Historians" have been used by Palestinian historians, for whom access to the Israeli archives is more problematic, and have served as the building blocks of what had already been the Palestinian historical narrative based on the recollections of the refugees. Most historians now agree that there was not a specific, detailed plan or an explicit order for the systematic expulsion of Palestinians, even if some individual local commanders interpreted Plan D in that way. However, in the view of Benny Morris, there was a consensus in support of the notion of population "transfer," which "conditioned the Zionist leadership, and below it, the officials and officers . . . with a mindset which was open to the idea and implementation of transfer and expulsion."[10]

One reason that the historical debate over the Arab exodus has been so intense is because it touches on the core of Israel's image of itself. Most Israeli commentators, whether historians or political leaders, were eager to portray Israel as the innocent victim, rather than the conqueror, in the events that took place from 1947 to 1949.

The War of 1948–49

On May 14, 1948, David Ben-Gurion proclaimed the birth of the new State of Israel, "a Jewish state established by and for the Jewish people." The next day, armed forces from Syria, Iraq, Transjordan, and Egypt entered Palestine. Consequently, the State of Israel was born in war and its first aim was survival.

Israel's War of Independence, as it is known in Israel, was to consist of three phases of fighting, interspersed by UN-sponsored ceasefires.

The First Phase of Fighting, May 15–June 10, 1948

In the south, an Egyptian army of ten thousand men crossed the border near the coast and attacked some isolated Jewish settlements in what was deemed to be part of the new Arab state. In the north, Syrian forces crossed the border but were resisted by Jewish settlers and Haganah forces, the latter now formed into the Israeli Defense Forces (IDF). Most of the invaders were compelled to withdraw. They lacked ammunition and were the least experienced of the Arab forces.

The major conflict was the battle for Jerusalem, just as it had been in the final days of the British Mandate. **Abdullah** of Transjordan moved his Arab Legion to defend the Old City, the mostly Arab East Jerusalem. It was his army that the Israelis wanted most to defeat, for two main reasons: first, they wanted to gain control of the Old City in order to protect the Jewish holy places and the Jewish minority that lived there; and, second, the Israelis knew that the Arab Legion was the most effective and best-trained Arab army – if they could defeat it, then the other Arab armies would collapse.

However, the Israelis were not able to overcome the Arab Legion, although they did gain control of West Jerusalem and were able to feed and protect the Jewish population in that part of the city. The Arab inhabitants fled or were forced out.

On June 10, the UN persuaded the warring parties to agree to a ceasefire. During the lull, the Israelis secured fresh supplies of weapons from Eastern Europe, mainly from the Czechs. (Britain had previously been the main supplier of arms to Egypt, Jordan, and Iraq but complied with the UN embargo on supplying arms to the warring sides.) The

Israelis also used the ceasefire to recruit more men and reorganise and rearm themselves. This gave them a significant advantage, and when the Egyptians broke the truce, the Israelis went on the offensive and seized the initiative from the Arab forces.

The Second Phase of Fighting, July 9–18, 1948

In the second phase of fighting, the Israeli priority was to try to widen the corridor leading to Jerusalem, taking land allocated to the Arabs in the process. They were particularly eager to control this territory to forestall any UN peace plan that might force them back to the borders that had been drawn in the 1947 partition plan. They were largely successful and, although the Arab Legion held the Old City of Jerusalem, it did not attempt to seize land allocated to the Jewish state.

In the south, the Israelis resisted further Egyptian advances in the Negev (see map on p. 76), while they took Nazareth in the north and several other Arab towns in the center. In the ten days of fighting during this second phase of the war, Israel improved its position and kept the upper hand for the rest of the war.

During the second truce, in September, Count Bernadotte, the special UN mediator from Sweden, produced a peace plan. It gave added land to the Arabs in the south and more land to the Israelis in the north, but Jerusalem was still to be an international city under UN control, and the Arab refugees were all to have the right to return home.

The next day, Bernadotte was assassinated by the Stern Gang. The new Israeli government wanted to maintain international support and ordered the dissolution of the Stern Gang and Irgun. Some of their members were then incorporated into the IDF.

The Third Phase of Fighting, October 15, 1948–January 1949

In mid-October, the Israelis broke the ceasefire and concentrated on defeating the Egyptians in the south. This they did, even pursuing the Egyptian Army over the border. Under US pressure, they agreed to withdraw from Egyptian territory, but they remained in complete control of the Negev Desert.

Meanwhile, in the north, Israeli forces completed their capture of the Galilee region, and according to Benny Morris, "IDF forces carried out at least nine massacres of Palestinian civilians and prisoners of war."[11] This followed the instructions of the local commander, who, after a meeting with Ben-Gurion, ordered his men to implement "a quick and immediate cleansing of the conquered areas."[12]

The Results of the War

A final ceasefire was arranged in January 1949. The new Israeli nation had lost six thousand lives, almost 1 percent of the entire Jewish population. However, the Israelis now controlled 78 percent of what had been the British Mandate of Palestine rather than the 55 percent allocated to the new state by the UN.

Furthermore, four hundred thousand Palestinian Arabs had fled between May 1948 and January 1949. Most ended up in Gaza or on land bordering the west bank of the Jordan River. This flight and the events of 1947–49 have become known in Arabic as the ***Nakba***, the catastrophe or disaster.

For the Israelis, this had been the war of national liberation. They had survived their first great test and were confident of their future as an independent nation. An American Zionist, Nahum Goldmann, wrote of the psychological effects of the Israeli victory:

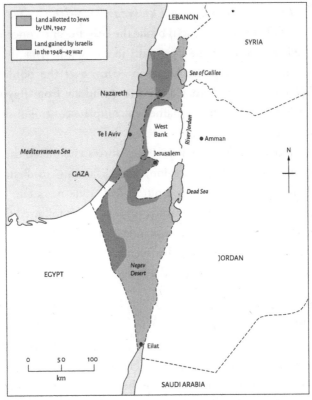

Israeli gains in the 1948–49 war

It seemed to show the advantages of direct action over negotiation and diplomacy … The victory offered such a glorious contrast to the centuries of persecution and humiliation, of adaptation and compromise, that it seemed to indicate the only direction that could possibly be taken from then on. To tolerate no attack . . . and shape history by creating facts so simple, so compelling, so satisfying that it became Israel's policy in its conflict with the Arab world.[13]

The lessons that Israel had learned, especially of the advantages of "direct action over negotiation and diplomacy" and to "shape history by creating facts," was to become particularly evident in Israeli policy in the years ahead.

Armistice Agreements

Between January and July 1949, armistice agreements were signed, under UN supervision, between Israel and each of the neighbouring Arab states.

1. The first agreement was between Israel and Egypt. It confirmed their prewar borders, while the Gaza area of Arab Palestine came under Egyptian military rule.

2. The second was between King Abdullah of Jordan and Israel. The king wanted his forces to keep control of the **West Bank**, the name given to the Palestinian Arab land west of the Jordan River. This area would now be governed as part of his kingdom. In this way, most of Arab Palestine, including the Old City of Jerusalem, now became part of the new, enlarged Kingdom of Jordan, as the state became known. The Israelis were eager to make peace with the king so that they could keep control of the newer, western part of Jerusalem. They preferred a partitioned Jerusalem to the international zone that the US and UN had wanted.

3. The third agreement was between Israel and Syria. When the fighting in the north ended, Syrian forces were in control of small pieces of territory that had been allocated to the new Jewish state. In July 1948, the UN negotiated that the Syrians would withdraw from the ceasefire lines if the vacated area became a demilitarised zone. This meant that Israel could not station any troops or weapons there. This agreement provided a buffer zone between the two sides.

The "Perpetual War"

The armistice agreements were supposed to lead to permanent peace treaties, but there was to be no such treaty between Israel and an Arab nation for nearly thirty years. The two key issues on which agreement could not be reached were borders and refugees.

Some Arab states were willing to negotiate over borders but all of them stuck to the policy on refugees formulated by the Arab League: Israel had created the problem, and as a result, the refugees had the "right to return" to their homes or to be compensated by Israel. Israel claimed that the Arabs had created the refugee problem by invading Israel and starting the war, and would only negotiate if it was agreed that most of the refugees should be settled *outside* Israel.

There were further obstacles to permanent peace. Public opinion in the Arab countries was intensely bitter over their defeat and in their hatred of Israel. Arabs viewed Israel as an outpost of Western colonialism in the heart of the Arab world. For the Israeli government, peace with its Arab neighbours was desirable but not worth the price of giving up any territory or agreeing to the return of large numbers of Palestinian refugees. Besides, the Israelis believed that time was on their side: rather than push for a peace based on the UN Partition Plan, the UN would get used to the new, expanded borders of the Israeli state and to the idea of a divided Jerusalem. In other words, Israel decided that it did not need permanent peace with the Arabs nor a solution to the Palestinian refugee problem. Its priorities were now to build the new state, implement large-scale Jewish immigration, and consolidate their independence.

How Did Israel Win the War?

There is dramatic variation in how historians have sought to explain the outcome of the First Arab-Israeli War. Put simply, there is the Zionist interpretation, which is still largely taught in Israeli schools today, and the revisionist interpretation.

In the last thirty years, historians have analyzed Israeli government documents from the time of the war. Foremost among them is the British-Israeli historian Avi Shlaim. This "new" history focuses on two main areas: the military balance between the two sides and the war aims of the Arabs.

The Zionist Interpretation

This interpretation maintains that the war was a struggle between tiny Israel and a huge Arab coalition made up of several armies. Israel was fighting for its own survival against Arab forces that were united in their aim of destroying the new state. Israel was the Jewish David fighting an Arab Goliath.

Israel had far fewer weapons, fewer soldiers, and was poorly equipped, and yet, against all the odds, it won the war through the heroic efforts, tenacity, and courage of its people. This is the popular, heroic interpretation. An example comes from Chaim Herzog, who was an army officer, diplomat, and later president of Israel:

> Israel's victory was the result of the self-sacrifice and determination of a people to fight for its existence. The spirit that animated its people and the courage it reflected were the function of a rare

form of determined and inspiring leadership ... David Ben-Gurion [was] a powerful, charismatic leader ... with sufficient courage to lead against the most impossible odds [despite] the disadvantages under which the Israeli Army operated during the War of Independence – its weakness in manpower [and] its lack of modern weapons.[14]

The Revisionist Interpretation

It is certainly true that at the start of the war in May 1948, the Israelis had only about thirty thousand soldiers and their weapons were inferior. But they built up the army to about sixty-five thousand by July and had nearly a hundred thousand in arms by December 1948. The total number of Arab troops involved in the fighting was similar at the start and was also built up during the war, but not as quickly as that of the Israelis.

In terms of weaponry, the Israelis were poorly equipped at the start but, particularly during the first truce in June to July 1948, they gained access to much more equipment from Europe and were better armed for the rest of the war. In short, the stronger side won.

The Israelis had other military advantages. About twenty-five thousand of them had fought in the British Army in the Second World War and gained valuable experience in training, organisation, and technology. The only Arab force that was as well trained and disciplined were the ten thousand men of the Arab Legion of Transjordan, which was partly financed by Britain and led by British officers.

War Aims

The Jews in Palestine, particularly under the leadership of Ben-Gurion, had long recognised that they would need to use force to establish their new state. The Palestinian Arabs, on the other hand, lacked strong and effective leadership and had no coordinated military force or embryonic state institutions.

The Palestinians did have the support of the neighbouring Arab states, even if their governments had only begun to plan for invasion at the last minute. King Abdullah of Transjordan claimed to be commander-in-chief. But the Arab leaders were far from united in their goals, and each tended to fight for their own interests, often to gain control of a piece of Palestinian territory for themselves. There was very little coordination of their efforts in the war. This was particularly evident in the third phase of fighting when none of Egypt's allies answered its appeal for help against Israeli forces. Furthermore, both the Egyptian and Syrian governments were deeply suspicious of King Abdullah's aims.

King Abdullah and the Israelis

The case of King Abdullah of Transjordan is particularly significant. Before the war, he had held a secret meeting with Golda Meir, one of the Palestinian Jewish leaders (and another future prime minister of Israel). He had let it be known that he did not think the Palestinian Arab state could survive on its own. He thought it would be too weak and he wished to attach it to his state. He saw himself as the leader of an enlarged Arab state (and, in this, he had some support from the British). He also assured Jewish leaders that he would *not* invade territory allocated to the new Jewish state. No actual agreements were made at this meeting, but a mutual understanding was established.

The Arab Legion was the most effective and well-trained Arab army.

When the war started, King Abdullah's Arab Legion advanced to defend the Old City of Jerusalem against the Israeli offensive and they held on to it throughout the war. Yet the Arab Legion made little effort to stop the Israelis from seizing West Jerusalem. Nor did the Legion invade the territory of the new Jewish state. Furthermore, the Arab Legion remained neutral when the Israelis fought Egyptian forces and ignored the latter's appeals for help in the second and third phases of the war.

In other words, the army from Transjordan invaded what was to be the new Arab state but it never invaded Jewish, Israeli territory. Its aim was to gain control of most of Arab Palestine (on the western side of the Jordan River), which it did, but not to destroy the State of Israel. Israel was able to exploit its understanding with Transjordan to break the chain of hostile Arab states, deepen the divisions in the Arab coalition, and pick off its Arab opponents one by one. The fact that Israel and Transjordan were "the best of enemies" is largely ignored in the heroic interpretation of the war.

In conclusion, most historians, including several Israeli ones, would now subscribe to the revisionist interpretation. However, few would doubt that the Israelis had shown a high degree of unity, discipline, and tenacity fighting for the survival of their newly independent state.

Personal Testimony
The Impact of the Second World War

Menachem Begin, leader of Irgun, writes on the impact of the Holocaust on the Zionist struggle for a Jewish state:

> [At the end of the Second World War] we viewed the whole situation in a totally different manner. We examined it from the viewpoint of the whole of Jewry. The extermination of Jews in Europe was in full swing. The gates of the Holy Land were barred to any who sought sanctuary ... The political situation required an intensification of the struggle ... To surrender would be to incur the double shame: of condoning extermination in Europe and enslavement in our homeland ... We saw our people in Europe in the endless procession of death; we saw the ghettos going up in flames; we saw the oppressor plotting against us all. And from down the corridors of history, we heard the echo of those other wars, the cursed internecine wars in dying Jerusalem nineteen centuries before.[15]

An Israeli Soldier's Recollection of the War

Mordecai Bar-On was an officer in the IDF during the 1948–49 War. In 2007, he wrote an article in which he explained his personal perspective:

> The nineteen-year-old native Palestinian Jew I was at the time . . . could see no alternative but to fight for my life and our national aspirations. Like all Jews in Palestine, I too burst onto the streets as soon as the UN General Assembly voted in favour of the establishment of a Jewish state and I too danced the night away drunk with joy. Early the next morning, my rifle and I escorted a bus en route to Tel Aviv. When we passed through the Arab village of Yazur, perched astride the road, we came under fire and the bus driver was wounded in the arm. This was the first act of violence I encountered, and it was clearly initiated by Arabs. A few weeks later, Elik Shamur, who commanded the station on the other side of the line, and six members of his squad were ambushed at the same spot and killed to a man. Had it been my turn to check the road, I would not now be writing these lines. Thus, from the perspective of my personal memory, the war, unequivocally, was the result of aggression on the part of Palestinian Arabs, who turned a short, peaceful drive from my home to Tel Aviv into a highly dangerous adventure.

It may be assumed that many young Jews of my generation in Palestine had similar experiences. In their minds, these memories firmly implanted the perception of how the war came about: as a result of the Arab refusal to accept the UN verdict and of Arab aggression, which endangered our lives in very real terms.

This has remained the way that Israel – through popular historiography and other means of commemoration – collectively remembers the story. These perceptions were not invented. Despite its bias, the Israeli narrative, which makes the Arabs the culprits in the violence, was not the result of manipulation but reflected the recurrent and very real experiences of numerous contemporary Israelis.[16]

The Events of 1948

Abu 'Arab, a shopkeeper living in Nazareth, recounted his story in 2007:

I was 12 when the Zionists occupied my land, when my village fell. Saffuriyyeh was a prosperous village … We had plenty of water and green fields which people farmed. Each family owned a bit of land to grow crops on. We had two schools, one for boys and the other for girls. There were three mosques and eight olive factories. We traded with nearby Nazareth and Haifa, selling them vegetables. Maybe four to five people served in the British Army under the Mandate; one was Ahmad-al-Tubi. They wore uniforms and owned cars, and some even had some guns. But, when the fighting with the Jews began, it was the peasants who led the resistance.

We came under air attack on the 16th day of the fasting month of Ramadan. The attacks came out of the blue and the ground shook with the explosions … We heard a plane flying overhead, and then the bombs began to fall.

The decision to leave under such ferocious and sustained attack was made so suddenly that we could snatch only a few belongings. As we fled up the hill, I looked back and all I could see was smoke. We knew the village had fallen, but the Palestinians did not give up elsewhere, because fighting continued in the north. Our parents were simple people and all they wanted was to protect their children. I don't blame them, but we have to continue fighting for our rights.

Along with hundreds of others, we walked north until we reached Bint Jbeil in Lebanon, where some of our relatives were waiting with blankets and food. We stayed there for 28 days, and then we boarded some buses which took us to an area called *Saha al-Hamra* ["the red square"] before going off to the Bekaa' [Valley], where we stayed in makeshift tents for 11 months before renting a house.[17]

CHAPTER 5

Palestinians and Israelis

1950s–60s

This chapter considers the impact of the diaspora (or dispersal) of Palestinian Arabs after 1949, the early development of the State of Israel, and the impact of Israel's wars with neighbouring Arab states on the Palestinians.

- **What happened to the Palestinians?**
- **How did Palestinian nationalism reemerge?**
- **How did the State of Israel develop?**
- **What was the impact of the wider Arab-Israeli conflict on the Palestinians?**

The Palestinian Diaspora

More than half of the Arab population of Palestine was displaced between 1947 and 1949 – over 700,000 people out of a total of 1.35 million. Most of these refugees went to the West Bank or Gaza, the parts of Palestine that were not incorporated into the new State of Israel. The rest went to neighbouring Arab countries such as Jordan, Syria, and Lebanon, some to states in the Persian Gulf, and a small number, especially among the more affluent and educated, to Europe or the United States. A few of the refugees went to live with relatives but the vast majority ended up living in tents in hastily constructed camps. After the establishment of the State of Israel, it became common to refer to the Arabs from Palestine as Palestinians.

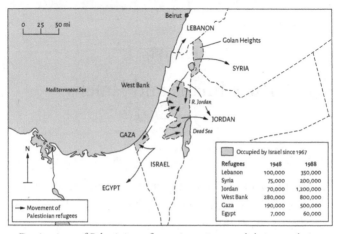

Destinations of Palestinian refugees in 1948–49 and their population growth by 1988

The Palestinians in the West Bank, whether refugees or not, came under the rule of King Abdullah, who now controlled the land on both the east and the west banks of the Jordan River. The Palestinians in the West Bank were offered Jordanian citizenship, as were the Palestinians who crossed the Jordan River.

The newly arrived refugees, whether on the west or east bank, could take up work and live outside the camps. In fact, the Jordanian government was eager to assimilate them: it did not want them to assert or demonstrate a separate Palestinian identity. They were to be Jordanians.

The refugees in Gaza came under Egyptian military rule and lived in a small, densely populated coastal area that became known as the Gaza Strip. Almost 80 percent of the population in Gaza were refugees. They lacked water and electricity and depended on handouts of food and money from different agencies. As in the West Bank, the people of Gaza, whether native Gazans or newly arrived refugees, were politically restricted and not allowed to form independent Palestinian organisations.

In Lebanon, Palestinian refugees were even more constrained by the local host community and were largely restricted to living and working within the limits of the camps. Those who moved to Syria were denied passports and the right to vote but could access education and government employment.

The Palestinians outside the new State of Israel were widely dispersed, fragmented, and traumatised. They were leaderless, too. The traditional leaders, the notables, were discredited, often blamed for the "loss" of Palestine. Many of the younger, middle-class leaders who emerged in the 1930s had been killed, deported, or forced to flee in the Revolt of 1936–39 or had fled in the *Nakba* of 1948–49.

To support the refugees in the camps of the West Bank, Gaza, and the Arab states, the **United Nations Relief and Works Agency (UNRWA)** was established in December 1948. It provided food, shelter, and clothing. UNRWA's resources were spread thinly and living conditions were harsh, as explained by Ghazi Daniel, a refugee, who remembered:

A few months after our arrival, we were penniless and had to move into a refugee camp with 2,000 other homeless Palestinians. It is beyond human endurance for a family of eleven to live in a small tent through all the seasons of the year on UNRWA rations. Fathers buried their children who died of hunger. Some buried their fathers who died of disease. On winter days we all crawled together to gain the warmth of humans.[1]

Today there are over five million UN-registered Palestinian refugees, mostly descendants of those who were made homeless in 1948–49.

The Arabs in Israel

The flight of Palestinians left only about 155,000 non-Jews within the borders of the new Israeli state. This was, for the Israeli government, a manageable number. From July 1948, it became official Israeli policy to oppose the return of refugees. Most of the refugees had left out of fear, to escape the fighting, or because they were expelled. However, the Israelis argued that the refugees were responsible for their own plight and should not be allowed to return.

The United Nations disagreed and, in December 1948, passed Resolution 194, which recognised the refugees' right to return or be offered compensation. Some did try to return, crossing the 1949 ceasefire lines to reclaim their property, harvest their crops, or see their relatives. A small minority carried out acts of sabotage and attacked Jews who had settled on their lands. All were classed by the Israelis as "infiltrators," and although perhaps twenty thousand did manage to return to their property or to nearby villages, about a thousand died in the attempt.

Altogether, about 350 Arab villages in the new state were depopulated in the period from late 1947 to January 1949 and the land was expropriated. This seizure of Arab land was carried out by the Israeli military, who were given the responsibility of managing the Palestinian population.

Most of the cities were emptied of Arabs, too. The Israelis resisted the UN call for the repatriation of the refugees: many Arab villages were destroyed, others handed over to Jewish kibbutzim. The 1950 Law of Absentees' Property defined abandoned Arab property as belonging to "absentees" who, by fleeing, had forfeited their right to the property. This included the property of Arabs who had only moved to a nearby village to escape the fighting.

The Israeli decision to keep refugees from returning to their land represents a decisive turning point in the development of the conflict, arguably more important than the actual expulsion in creating the Palestinian refugee problem. Uri Avnery, an Israeli who fought in the 1948 War and later became a peace activist, firmly believed that the decision "not to allow the 750,000 Arab refugees to return to their homes" was what did the most to determine "the subsequent history of the conflict."[2]

Much Arab land was allocated to recent Jewish immigrants, especially in border areas where the new inhabitants could act as auxiliary security forces and deter Arabs from returning to their villages. The Israelis were particularly motivated to populate these parts because of the fear that UN pressure might force Israel to hand back land taken during the war in a final peace agreement.

The Arabs who remained in Israel became Israeli citizens and constituted about 15 percent of the total Israeli population. They were variously known as Israeli Arabs or Palestinian Israelis. They continued to be subject to dispossession and displacement, usually in the name of security because they were seen by the Israelis as a threat, a potentially subversive element.

From 1949 to 1952, a further forty Palestinian villages were depopulated, and their inhabitants moved to other villages. Many Israeli Arabs lived near the borders, often in areas that had been declared military zones. In these zones, they could, under the orders of the military, be banished and have their properties confiscated. Whole villages could be cleared of their inhabitants. Some were deported to the West Bank or Gaza, but thousands became "internal refugees."

Even those who held on to their land found that the state limited their supplies of water and electricity. Many left the land and became casual labourers, often doing seasonal work for low pay. Another form of discrimination resulted from the fact that Israeli Arabs were not eligible to do military service: access to certain government jobs, housing, and social security benefits was closed to those who had not completed it.

Confused and disoriented, they were also isolated from the Arab world. They lacked any effective leadership, especially as many of the most educated, professional Palestinians had left. Furthermore, Arabs in Israel were subject to military rule from 1950 to 1966. Their movement was severely curtailed by checkpoints, curfews, and the need for travel permits. They were a marginalised group in a country where Jewish immigrants became citizens of a nation-state that was made by them and for them.

The Reemergence of Palestinian Nationalism

Most Palestinian refugees yearned, and expected, to return to their original homes: living on UN support was to be temporary. However, the UN policy of repatriation was not implemented because of insufficient international pressure on Israel to do so. In the years to come, Israel was to absorb nearly half a million Jews from Arab states, as explained on p. 98, and to insist that the Arab states should resettle the Palestinian refugees.

Camps run by UNRWA became home for most Palestinian refugees. In time, tents were replaced with mud huts and concrete buildings, and schools were established. The conditions in the camps in Gaza were described by General Burns, chief of staff of the UN forces, in the 1950s:

They live in little huts of mud and concrete blocks, corrugated iron roofs, row after row. Fairly adequate medical service is provided, probably better than was enjoyed before they were expelled from their native villages. Children swarm everywhere. There are primary schools for nearly all of them. There are secondary schools for many of the adolescents. And what will these youths and girls do when they have finished their secondary school training? There is no employment for them in the Strip, and very few can leave it to work elsewhere. The Gaza Strip resembles a vast concentration camp. They can look to the east and see wide fields, once Arab land, cultivated extensively by a few Israelis.[3]

Most refugees remained poor and unemployed. In the camps, they formed a ring of human misery around the borders of Israel. Crowded together, they became frustrated and bitter.

Not surprisingly, it was in the camps that Palestinian nationalism found its strongest support. Yet it did not gather significant backing for some time, and many have characterised the period from 1949 to the mid-1960s as the "lost years" of Palestinian nationalism. Certainly, it took many years for the Palestinians – defeated, displaced, and stateless – to acknowledge the extent of the disaster that had befallen them, while physical survival was their overriding preoccupation.

However, the period following the *Nakba* were not wholly "lost years": the disaster indirectly strengthened Palestinian nationalism and gave impetus to the struggle of the Palestinians to regain their homeland. The shared experience of exile, whether in the refugee camps of the West Bank, Gaza,

Syria, Lebanon, and Jordan, or further afield, was to shape and cement Palestinian identity. It instilled, particularly for those in the refugee camps, a determination not to be "resettled" permanently but to "return" to their homes. Many kept (and their descendants still do) the keys to the houses from which they were expelled in 1948, resolved to return and reclaim their property one day.

The dispossessed, exiled Palestinians were not lacking in champions, as several Palestinian nationalist movements emerged. The leading organisation prior to the mid-1960s was the Movement for Arab Nationalism (MAN), which was founded by Palestinians in Lebanon in 1952. Its prime aim was the liberation of Palestine, but its members believed this could only be achieved with the support of regular troops from Arab nations and that the chief prerequisite was Arab unity. To achieve this, they looked to **President Gamal Abdel Nasser of Egypt**, as did millions across the Arab world. He was seen as the undisputed leader of the Arabs, the one who could unite them against Israel.

The leadership of MAN was highly committed and came from a younger generation. It established branches in Syria, Jordan, Iraq, and Yemen. However, it was bedeviled by infighting and, although it carried out a limited number of armed incursions into Israel, it never attained mass support.

There were many other Palestinian groups that tapped nationalist feeling in the 1950s and early 1960s and some of them carried out attacks inside Israel, especially from Gaza. However, Palestinian activists in Gaza were severely curbed by the Egyptian military authorities, as were those in other "host" countries, especially Lebanon and Jordan, whose governments feared Israeli retaliation in response to Palestinian attacks.

The Rise of Fatah

Out of all the Palestinian groups, it was **Fatah** that was to become the preeminent symbol of Palestinian nationalism and assume leadership of the movement. (The Arabic initials of its name "the Movement for the Liberation of Palestine," spells *fatah*, or victory, when read in reverse.)

Yasser Arafat, leader of Fatah

Fatah originated in the early 1950s among Palestinian students in Cairo. One of their number, **Yasser Arafat**, reorganised the Palestinian Students' Union. According to a fellow student, Salah Khalaf, Arafat had two strong convictions from the start: "that the Palestinians could expect nothing from the Arab regimes . . . [and] that the Palestinians could rely only on themselves."[4] These beliefs were to form the foundations of Fatah ideology. Beginning in 1954, Fatah began carrying out minor attacks on Israel from Gaza.

Arafat, Khalaf, and their colleagues left Cairo after graduation, some of them finding work in Kuwait, where they made contact with other Palestinian activists. Fatah, for whom Arafat was always "first among equals,"[5] was able to build up a network of Palestinian supporters, mostly professionals and businessmen, in the Gulf and in Lebanon, Syria, Jordan, and other Arab countries.

When Fatah was formally established in 1959, its founders agreed that a tight structure was necessary to maintain secrecy in the planning of guerrilla operations. Above all, however, what bound Fatah together was the focus on the goal of liberating Palestine by armed struggle. For Fatah, the liberation of the homeland took priority over the achievement of Arab unity.

Several factors were to help Fatah emerge, even if not until the late 1960s, as the leading Palestinian nationalist organisation. First, the newspaper *Filastinuna* ("Our Palestine"), which was published regularly in the early 1960s, reached the refugees in the camps and Palestinians in the wider diaspora. It acknowledged the desperately poor conditions in which camp dwellers lived. Its "Palestine first" message struck a chord with the powerless, stateless refugees and gave heart and hope to their yearning to "return" home. Many of Fatah's recruits came from the camps.

Second, disillusionment and impatience with the Arab regimes set in. In 1964, when the leaders of thirteen Arab states met in Cairo, President Nasser announced that he had no immediate plan to liberate Palestine. Like the leaders of other Arab regimes, many of whom seemed more concerned with building their own states, he was reluctant to provoke the military might of Israel. Arab unity seemed more distant than ever.

At their meeting in Cairo, the Arab leaders established the Palestine Liberation Organization (PLO), led by Ahmed Shuqairy, a Palestinian ally of Nasser's. Its formation may have been an attempt to show a united Arab front, and was perhaps also a concession designed to rein in Palestinian activists.

Not surprisingly, most Palestinian groups were critical of this move. Fatah was still focused on using armed struggle to liberate Palestine, but it did recognise the need for support from the Arab regimes, especially those of the "host" countries.

This was particularly the case for Syria, where some of Fatah's forces were being trained for military action.

Fatah's Military Operations

In 1964, Fatah decided to launch guerrilla operations against Israel. The first operation was carried out, unannounced, in December 1964. Then, on January 1, 1965, Fatah called for the start of the armed struggle. The effect in the refugee camps was instantaneous:

> Palestinians in the camps received this news with joy, and after it the situation in the camps changed. Everybody started talking about this new step, and their desire to participate – especially the students and young workers.[6]

Armed raids against Israeli military targets, of which Fatah claimed there were thirty-nine in 1965, were little more than an irritant to Israel with its vastly superior armed forces. The raids resulted in harsh retaliatory measures, including the bombing of the camps in which Fatah were believed by the Israeli military to have their bases. Furthermore, when the Israelis hit West Bank villages and refugee camps, the inhabitants were rarely defended by the Jordanian Army, nor were they allowed to form their own defence militias.

However, Fatah's call for armed struggle acted as a rallying cry for many Palestinians in the diaspora. Its call to arms was rooted in the experience of a people who had been disarmed in 1936–39, in 1948–49, and in the camps.

Such factors help to explain why many Palestinians, especially the young men in the camps, responded to Fatah's call and were willing to become **fedayeen** ("those who sacrifice themselves"). Popular armed resistance did little to weaken the State of Israel but it evoked memories of the heroic, armed struggle of al-Qassam in 1936 and illustrated what, to many, was the "correct" path of popular, armed resistance. One of their leaders later reported that Fatah attracted strong, popular support "in '65 when we started our military action. Then the people realized that we were not just another movement, talking like the others."[7]

A major turning point, in terms of Fatah's growth, profile, and reputation, came in 1967. But first, it is necessary to understand how Israel developed in its first two decades.

Jewish Immigration and the Economic Development of Israel

When the State of Israel was created in 1948, it had a population of about 750,000, of which more than 80 percent were Jewish. Within four years, the Jewish population was to double.

Surrounded by hostile Arab states, Israel needed massive immigration both for its security and its development into a strong, modern state. In 1950, the **Law of Return** granted any Jew in the world the right to become a citizen of Israel.

Some of the earliest immigrants were survivors of the Holocaust: about 120,000, mostly from Poland, arrived in Israel. However, the majority of immigrants in the first few years were Arabic-speaking Jews from Arab countries. In many of the big Arab cities in the Middle East, such as Cairo, Damascus, and Baghdad, there were large Jewish communities. They had lived there for centuries; many had prospered and very few of them were Zionist or had any desire to be uprooted and move to Israel.

Jews from Yemen immigrating to Israel in 1950. The Law of Return granted any Jew in the world the right to become a citizen of Israel.

However, the new state launched a campaign to persuade them to come to Israel and, after the 1948–49 War, Arab governments and people increasingly viewed them with suspicion as potential Zionists, associating them with what they saw as disaster in Palestine. Thus, under duress, about 120,000 Iraqi Jews moved to Israel in the early 1950s, as well as smaller numbers from Egypt, Yemen, and other Arab states. In the mid-1950s, 165,000 arrived from Morocco. These Middle Eastern and North African Jews were known as **Mizrahi Jews**.

Most Mizrahi Jews had been forced to leave their belongings behind and consequently arrived in Israel with few possessions. Many were settled on land and in houses recently abandoned by Palestinian Arabs and confiscated by the Israelis. Thousands were housed in so-called development towns, often in border areas where the new Jewish immigrants might provide a buffer zone to act as a deterrent against attempts by Palestinian refugees to cross into Israel and retake their lands.

Immigration on this scale presented a huge challenge to the new Israeli state. The new arrivals not only had to be housed and educated, they also had to be integrated into what was a predominantly European culture. They had not experienced the Holocaust, nor had they grown up in the *Yishuv*, the Jewish community in British-ruled Palestine, which was largely made up of Jews from Eastern Europe. The Mizrahi Jews were generally poorer and less well educated. Seen as a source of cheap labour, they took the poorest-paid jobs and often suffered discrimination.

However, the most marginalised group were undoubtedly the Arabs living in Israel – the Palestinian Israelis. They were also regarded with suspicion because of the continuing conflict with the Arab states on Israel's borders.

Building the State of Israel

Immigrants to Israel were discouraged from speaking Arabic, Yiddish, Russian, English, or any other language of their country of origin. Instead, they were taught Hebrew. This ancient language was revived and adapted for modern usage and even developed its own slang. The Hebrew language played a crucial role in state building and in the development of an Israeli-Hebraic culture.

Equally, if not more, important in developing the Israeli state was the army. This is hardly surprising, as the Israelis had lived with the threat of invasion since the end of the war in 1949. They were convinced that the neighbouring Arab states would try to attack again. The IDF would have to be constantly on the alert.

Men had to do two years of military service and women one year. They had to spend long periods in the reserves so that Israel had an increasingly large pool of men and women ready to take up arms and defend the country. The Israeli Army not only defended the new nation but also helped to shape it. The Jews of Israel had come from Europe, the United States, the Middle East, and North Africa. In the army, the young, newly arrived Jews all received similar training, lived together, and had to learn Hebrew. This experience probably did more than anything else to shape the newly arrived Jews into Israelis.

Israel became richer, stronger, and more highly developed in the 1950s and 1960s. Large areas were irrigated and cultivated, often with citrus fruits. New industries, such as chemicals and defence, were built up and Israel became a manufacturer of military equipment. Huge sums of money were spent on the armed forces to defend the country.

The high level of education and skills of many Israeli citizens played a major part in Israel's economic development, as did the availability of a plentiful supply of cheap immigrant labour. With an increasingly large proportion of its population living in towns and cities and working in service industries, Israel enjoyed a rising standard of living and became more and more like a Western European state.

The speed of Israel's progress would not have been possible without finance from abroad. In the early years, most of this aid came from Jews in the diaspora, especially from Zionist groups in the US. From 1952 onward, the state of West Germany started paying reparations – a sum of $715 million, to be paid over many years, was agreed. This was the equivalent of many billions in today's currency. After 1967, the US government also pumped in an increasingly large amount of aid – more than $2 billion a year by 1979. About 40 percent of this was economic aid and 60 percent came in the form of military equipment.

A sidewalk cafe on Ibn Gvirol Street in Tel Aviv, 1970

Israel was and remains a Jewish state. The concepts of Judaism, the Jewish people, and of *Eretz* Israel, which had been so important in the development of the *Yishuv*, continued to dominate the political life of the new state. From the start, the rabbis were granted full responsibility for marriage and divorce among Jews and for the laws regarding the observance of the Sabbath through their courts.

Religion was also to play an increasingly significant part in the politics of the new nation. In elections for the Israeli parliament, the **Knesset**, all of Israel was treated as one constituency and parliamentary seats were allocated to parties in proportion to the number of votes cast for them. (At present, any party that secures 5 percent of the vote is assured a seat in the Knesset.) Not surprisingly, this system of proportional representation sustained many parties. The parties reflected the wide range of backgrounds from which Israel's citizens came, with some of them being religiously oriented.

Politics in Israel was dominated by Mapai (in 1968, it was to merge with two smaller parties to form the Israeli Labor Party). It was led by David Ben-Gurion, the first prime minister of Israel, who towered over Israeli political life until his retirement in 1963. However, neither Mapai nor any other political party ever secured an overall majority.

All Israeli governments have therefore been coalition governments. Most have been made up of several parties, with the religious parties often holding the balance of power. These parties, largely representing Orthodox Jews, have consistently gained about 15 percent of the vote and have been able to extract huge concessions from the main party in government in return for their backing. Thus, they have won financial support from the state for religious schools, exemption from military service for Orthodox Jews, and the establishment of a Ministry of Religion. Increasingly, they have demanded that the state be governed by religious law.

The Arab-Israeli Conflict in the 1950s and 1960s

In the 1950s, the Israeli-Palestinian conflict was subsumed into the wider Arab-Israeli conflict in the region. There were no peace treaties between Israel and neighbouring Arab states: the Arabs refused to recognise Israel and Israel refused to allow more than a few thousand displaced Palestinians to return to their lands in what was now the State of Israel.

The 1950s was generally a time of great instability in the Arab world: the rulers of Egypt, Syria, and Iraq, discredited by their defeat in the 1948–49 War, were swept away. This defeat intensified the Arabs' anger and the desire to avenge their humiliation at the hands of Israeli forces.

With Israel surrounded by hostile Arab states, Prime Minister Ben-Gurion was determined to demonstrate Israeli military power to force the Arab states to accept Israel's existence, show that no attack from their lands would go unpunished, and pressure the Arab states into curbing cross-border raids. To this end, Israel used disproportionate force in responding to raids by Palestinian fedayeen, most of whom came from the West Bank or Egyptian-controlled Gaza.

One such reprisal took place in October 1953. After the killing of an Israeli woman and her two children in a Palestinian grenade attack, Israeli forces entered the West Bank village of Qibya and killed sixty-nine of its inhabitants, most of them women and children.

The Suez War, 1956

Another particularly significant Israeli reprisal raid occurred in 1955. Operation Black Arrow saw an attack on an Egyptian military post in Gaza in which thirty-eight Egyptian soldiers were killed. (Both this raid and the one on Qibya were led by future Israeli prime minister **Ariel Sharon**.) This incident set off a series of events that led to the Suez War of 1956.

The new Egyptian leader, President Nasser, felt humiliated by the Israeli attack and sought to buy arms to build up his country's defences in the face of Israeli military superiority. Rebuffed by the United States, he secured weapons from communist Czechoslovakia, an ally of the Soviet Union. Angered by this move and fearful that Egypt was siding with the Soviet Union, the opponent of the West in the **Cold War**, the United States and Britain decided to teach Nasser a lesson and bring him to heel. They canceled their loans to Egypt for the building of the Aswan Dam, a huge irrigation and hydroelectrical project and, for Nasser, a symbol of the new, dynamic Egypt he wanted to build. The Egyptian leader then stunned the West by nationalizing the Anglo-French-owned Suez Canal. In response, the British and French conspired with the Israelis to invade Egypt.

The Israelis invaded Egypt, advancing across the Sinai Peninsula toward the Suez Canal (see the image on p. 106 for location), while the British and French bombed Egyptian airfields and landed troops. As it turned out, huge international pressure led to the invasion being called off after nine days. This was particularly humiliating for Britain and France as the most resolute opposition of all came from the United States. The US government believed that the Anglo-French action would alienate Arab states at a time when the US was eager to make friends in the Arab world to prevent any extension of Soviet influence in the region. The Middle East was now decidedly embroiled in the politics of the Cold War.

The Suez War had little direct impact on the Palestinians. The Israelis proved their military prowess in the speed with which they overran the Egyptian forces, but they were prevailed upon by the United States to withdraw. Surprisingly, for Nasser, it was a political victory: he had defied the European powers that had for so long dominated the Middle East and he had gained control of the Suez Canal.

However, Nasser's status as champion of the Arab world would eventually lead him into another war with Israel that, this time, led to a crushing defeat and to dramatic consequences for the Palestinians.

The Six-Day War, 1967

Amid increasing tension on the Israel-Syria border in 1966–67, Nasser was goaded by his Arab allies, especially Syria, into adopting increasingly warlike, anti-Israeli rhetoric. He took several steps to impress Arab public opinion and then, in May 1967, in the words of the historian Avi Shlaim, "What he did was to embark on an exercise in brinkmanship that was to carry him over the brink."

Nasser closed the Straits of Tiran, which cut off Israeli shipping from the Red Sea, the Indian Ocean, and the Far East. A week later, he called on Israel to give up the land taken in the 1948–49 War. The next day, **King Hussein of Jordan** signed a defence treaty with Egypt. He had come under intense pressure from his people, half of whom were Palestinian.

These actions provoked Israel into launching a preemptive strike. At dawn on the morning of Monday, June 5, 1967, Israel carried out air strikes that wiped out nearly all of the air forces of Egypt, Syria, and Jordan. With total air superiority achieved on the first day, Israel was able to take control of Egypt's Sinai and Syria's Golan Heights within six days (see below).

For the Palestinians, what was most devastating was that, in those six days, Israeli forces also seized Gaza (from Egypt) and the West Bank (from Jordan) so that, at the end of the war, Israel controlled all of what had been Mandatory Palestine. The map of the Middle East had been redrawn.

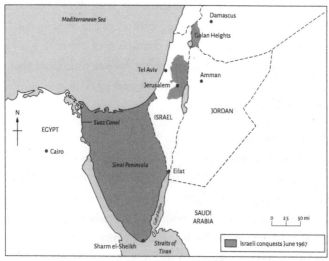

Territories occupied by Israel after the Six-Day War

The Aftermath of the Six-Day War

The Israelis had achieved an overwhelming military victory. Although the Arab forces of Egypt, Syria, and Jordan had larger armies, they were unprepared, and their air forces were destroyed on the first day. The Arab states had modern Soviet missiles and other weaponry, but the Israelis had over two hundred French fighter planes that had proved decisive. The Israelis were highly skilled and well trained, and they believed they were fighting for their nation's survival.

Now that they were the dominant power in the Middle East, the Israelis saw no need to hurry into peace negotiations. The Arab states, for their part, felt more hostile than ever. They blamed their defeat on the United States, France, and Britain, whom they accused of helping Israel in the war. At a conference of the Arab League in August 1967, the Arab leaders declared, "No peace with Israel, no recognition of Israel, no negotiation with it. We insist on the rights of the Palestinian people in their country."

UN Resolution 242

In November 1967, the United Nations Security Council unanimously passed Resolution 242, which called for permanent peace based on:

- "the withdrawal of Israeli armed forces from territories occupied in the recent conflict."
- respect for the right of every state in the area "to live in peace within secure and recognized boundaries, free from threats or acts of force."

The Resolution supported the Arabs on the issue of land and supported Israel on the issue of peace and security. Egypt and Jordan (although not Syria) accepted the Resolution, effectively recognising Israel's right to exist. Israel held up the "three nos" of the Arab League Conference in August as proof that the Arabs did not really want a peace settlement, but the Israeli government eventually accepted the Resolution in May 1968.

The UN led discussions with the warring parties but made little progress. Israel found that its occupation of Arab land gave it added security, while the Arabs insisted on Israeli withdrawal as a first step to peace and a token of Israeli good faith.

Many subsequent peace discussions were to be based on the formula of "land for peace," by which Israel would give up conquered Arab land in return for Arab recognition of Israel's right to exist and live in peace. Most notably, such discussions led to a peace treaty between Israel and Egypt in 1979.

The Yom Kippur War, 1973

In October 1973, six years after the Six-Day War, the Egyptian and Syrian governments resolved to regain the lands they had lost in 1967. Their military forces caught the Israelis completely by surprise.

On the day of Yom Kippur, the holiest day of the Jewish year, the forces attacked Israeli troops occupying Sinai and the Golan Heights in a secretly coordinated attack. They forced the Israelis to retreat and destroyed several hundred Israeli tanks.

However, within days, the Israelis recovered and launched a counterattack. Helped by a massive airlift of arms from the US, they drove the Arab armies back, and by the time the UN arranged a ceasefire, the Israelis had regained control of Sinai and the Golan Heights, as well as additional territory.

Nevertheless, the Arab armies had, in the initial stages of the war, shattered the Israelis' image of invincibility and restored Arab pride after the humiliation of the Six-Day War. Six years later, in 1979, Israel signed a peace treaty with Egypt, and Israeli forces were later withdrawn from Sinai.

Much of the world applauded this breakthrough to peace as Egypt became the first Arab state to recognise Israel. However, the Palestinians felt more vulnerable and exposed to an expansionist Israel than ever. The Israelis may have withdrawn from Sinai to gain recognition from Egypt, but they remained more determined than ever to maintain their control over the West Bank and Gaza.

Personal Testimony

A Palestinian Refugee

Salah Salah remembers his life in Galilee, in northern Palestine, before 1948 and then in exile:

> We kept good relations with the neighboring Arab Jews, with whom we used to trade. There was no hostility to speak of at the beginning but clashes erupted when we could no longer resolve the disputes over land and when some outside Jews began to appear in large numbers and with arms . . . then everything was turned upside down when we started hearing news

of villages falling and people running away [in 1948]. When we heard that Tiberias had fallen, followed by Safad [both towns are in the Galilee region], we began to have doubts about our ability to fight back and to protect ourselves. It was then that the decision to leave was taken to protect the people. We left to a village called al-Rameh and from there to Lebanon. The scenes of departure are unforgettable because there were many people walking in different directions, overlapping, crossing each other, but all leaving. It was a massive exodus.

In those early day as refugees, we felt ashamed, frustrated and dispossessed, so the idea that we, as young people, could motivate others was uplifting and liberating. Those were the 1950s when I was a young man who wanted to confront defeat and move on. I had this absolute commitment to organise and motivate people, so we started forming youth clubs in secret and it was through the need to reach out to others that we began to go to other places … The mobilization was necessary because, at that time, there was talk of the Palestinian problem as a refugee problem and there were all these proposals for naturalization and settlement of the refugees, even in remote parts of the Arab world. We did not have much money, but we felt the people were behind us. It was a period of real struggle and clean revolution.[8]

The Israeli Army General

Moshe Dayan spoke at the funeral of a young Israeli security guard who was killed while patrolling the Israeli-Gaza border. He is clear and honest in his understanding of why Palestinians might hate Israelis and why, in his opinion, Israelis could not afford to let their guard down. They would always have to be prepared to use force to preserve what they had won by force:

> Yesterday at dawn Roy was murdered ... Let us not cast blame today on the murderers. What can we say against their terrible hatred of us? For eight years now, they have sat in the refugee camps of Gaza and have watched how, before their very eyes, we have turned their land and villages, where they and their forefathers previously dwelled, into our home. It is not among the Arabs of Gaza, but in our own midst that we must seek Roy's blood. How did we shut our eyes and refuse to look squarely at our fate and see, in all its brutality, the fate of our generation?
>
> Let us today take stock of ourselves. We are a generation of settlement, and without the steel helmet and the gun's muzzle, we will not be able to plant a tree and build a house. Let us not fear to look squarely at the hatred that consumes and fills the lives of hundreds of Arabs who live around us. Let us not drop our gaze, lest our arms weaken. That is the fate of our generation. This is our choice, to be ready and armed, tough and hard – or else the sword shall fall from our hands and our lives will be cut short.[9]

CHAPTER 6

The Israeli Occupation of the Palestinian Territories

To understand the impact of the Israeli conquest of the West Bank and Gaza in 1967, three questions must be addressed:

- Why was Jerusalem, but not the rest of the occupied territories, annexed?
- How were the West Bank and Gaza administered?
- How and why did the Israelis build settlements in the West Bank and Gaza?

The West Bank and Gaza

Israel's dramatic victory in the Six-Day War presented its government with the issue of what to do with the occupied Palestinian territories of the West Bank and Gaza. How were they to be administered?

On one particular point the Israelis were united. They had taken control of the Old City of East Jerusalem and they were determined to hold on to it. As the Israeli defence minister, Moshe Dayan, said on the radio, "We have unified Jerusalem, the divided capital of Israel. We have returned to the holiest of our holy places, never to part from it again."[1]

The Israeli government proceeded to **annex** East Jerusalem. This act violated international law, and the United Nations General Assembly condemned it. Many of the city's Palestinian inhabitants were either evicted or offered money to leave after signing documents relinquishing their right to return. Arab housing was demolished to reconstruct the Jewish Quarter in the Old City. Furthermore, Israel confiscated a large swath of land to the east of the city that would, in time, form a barrier of Israeli settlements surrounding the city, thus cutting off the Palestinian

Victorious Israeli soldiers at the Western Wall in Jerusalem, June 1967

population of Jerusalem from its West Bank hinterland.[2]

While Israel was swift to annex East Jerusalem and declare Jerusalem the capital of Israel, its government held lengthy discussions on what policy to adopt for the rest of the West Bank and Gaza. The circumstances were very different from those at the end of Israel's first war with the neighbouring Arab states.

In 1949, the land the Israelis controlled had largely been cleared of its Palestinian Arab population and the minority who remained were deemed few enough to be incorporated into the new state and granted citizenship. By contrast, in June 1967, most Arabs were not displaced from the West Bank and Gaza during the fighting. In fact, over one million remained, far too many to be incorporated into Israel if it was to remain a predominantly Jewish state.

Thus, annexation and the granting of rights to Arabs as Israeli citizens were ruled out by the government. Israel wanted to remain in overall control of the land and exploit its resources, but it did not wish to bear the responsibility for the people of that land.

Israeli Military Administration

Policy on the ground was largely shaped by the Defense Ministry. Responsibility for the administration of the **Occupied Palestinian Territories (OPTs)**, as they came to be known, was vested in a military government. Defense Minister Dayan wished to preempt unrest and resistance and limit Israeli responsibility for, and the expense of, administering the Palestinian population. He therefore decided to adopt a policy of "normalization," to restore civilian life to what it had been as soon as possible and to make the "occupation invisible."[3]

Use of the Jordanian currency, the dinar, was continued alongside that of the Israeli shekel, and communication between the Arabs of the West Bank and Gaza and those in both Israel and neighbouring Jordan was allowed. Most mayors and *mukhtars* (village elders) were kept in place to maintain a sense of continuity and in the hope of maintaining strong local Palestinian leadership, as opposed to one dominated by the PLO. However, as Israeli historian Tom Segev has shown, the Israeli military presence in the West Bank developed into a huge bureaucracy that "invented more and more reasons to interfere in the residents' daily lives," producing laws and regulations that "reflected no clear policy or a calculated strategy but, rather, above all, arbitrariness."[4]

Nowhere was this "arbitrariness" more in evidence than in the Israeli permit regime by which the military government sought to regulate all aspects of daily life. Permits were required of Palestinians to open a business or to practice law or medicine, register or gain a license to drive a car, build a house, install a water pump or sink a well, plant olive or citrus trees, or live outside the area in which they were registered. In this way, even the most basic human rights (shelter, a livelihood, freedom of movement) became privileges that could be taken away. Permits were also required to publish or distribute newspapers, along with leaflets or posters of "political significance."

Furthermore, the granting of a permit, which might take years, could also be made conditional on the applicant's willingness to collaborate, such as by informing on neighbours. Not surprisingly, the permit regime contributed to the fragmentation of Palestinian society, eroding trust and sowing suspicion among its members as well as creating intense resentment toward Israeli forces.

Moreover, despite Israel's proclaimed early attempt to "normalise" conditions in the West Bank, the government implemented policies that prevented the development of a viable Palestinian economy, and certainly the foundations of a viable Palestinian political entity. The "open bridges" policy, often attributed to Dayan, may have allowed for free movement of people (and, initially, of goods), which enabled Palestinians from the West Bank and Gaza to visit their places of origin in Israel and led to an improved standard of living in the West Bank, but it also facilitated the incorporation of the West Bank's economy into that of Israel.

A de facto customs union gave Israeli products free access to the Palestinian market, but restrictions were placed on the movement of Palestinian manufactured goods into Israel. Agriculture suffered not only from subsidised Israeli competition but also from restrictions placed on Palestinian farmers' access to water. Many left their land to work as wage labourers in Israel.

By the mid-1980s, Palestinians from the occupied territories, together with Palestinian citizens of Israel, provided 50 percent of the labour in agriculture and construction in Israel. The West Bank and Gaza became a source of cheap labour as well as a captive consumer market for Israeli goods. In these ways, the West Bank and Gaza were made increasingly dependent on Israel.

The Israelis were eager to show that they were upholding international law, in particular the Hague Convention, which stipulates that an occupying power should recognise the laws in force in the territory before occupation.[5] As long as they did not contradict their own military orders, a combination of Ottoman, British, and Jordanian laws were used to enforce obedience and stifle resistance. For instance, the Israeli military government used an Ottoman law that allowed them to appropriate land that had not been cultivated for three consecutive years, while British emergency regulations were used to impose house searches, curfews, arrests and torture, administrative detention (imprisonment without charge or trial), deportation, and house demolitions.

Settlement Building

After months of deliberation, a policy of building settlements to house Jewish-Israeli civilians in occupied territory was pursued. Most members of the Labor-led coalition government agreed that settlements created "facts on the ground," which enhanced Israel's security. However, they disagreed on whether these might be used later as bargaining pieces in any peace negotiations.

For many of the more ideologically or religiously committed members of the government, settlements created a permanent foothold. For instance, Menachem Begin, former leader of Irgun, who would later form and lead the Likud Party, championed Israel's national right to annex all of historic Palestine, thus restoring *Eretz* Israel and implementing the Zionist idea in its entirety.

There was a fairly wide consensus on the need to establish a buffer zone that could shield Israel against attack from Jordan in the east. To that end, a strip of land along the entire length of the West Bank of the Jordan River was seized. Initially it was occupied by the military, then later by civilian settlements, both to bolster Israel's defence and to exploit the fertile land for commercial purposes.

Settlement building was portrayed to the rest of the world as necessary for "security" reasons because, under international law, military personnel can be deployed in occupied land. However, international law also stipulates that an "Occupying Power shall not . . . transfer parts of its own civilian population into the territory it occupies."[6]

Policy for the rest of the Occupied Territories did not proceed according to any one agreed-upon plan – far from it. Members of the government strongly disagreed on what to do. The actual process of settlement building emerged piecemeal, often the result of factional infighting within government circles. Policies were driven by interest groups or particular ministers rather than by a clear strategy. However, the permit regulations and the acts of confiscating Palestinian land and building settlements and roads all created "a certain dynamic that helped shape Israel's policy choices over the years."[7]

A variety of legal and bureaucratic means were exploited to justify the seizure of land, such as declaring it to be: "absentee property"; belonging to a hostile state (used to justify the establishment of fifteen settlements in the Jordan Valley); necessary for military purposes or for public needs, such as building roads to link settlements; or just simply state property. And land was not the only resource of which the military took control. The plentiful water aquifers of the West Bank were exploited for the use, both agricultural and domestic, of those living in Israel and the settlements. Such access for Palestinians was restricted.

Yitzhak Rabin, who became prime minister in 1974, was as determined as any of his predecessors to achieve Israel's security. To do so, he was willing to contemplate a Jordanian–Palestinian state on parts of the West Bank in which the Palestinians would have limited self-rule. Proposals were put to the Jordanians for an Israeli withdrawal from Jericho, near the border with Jordan, and the establishment of a Jordanian administration there – the so-called Jordanian option.

However, Rabin came under pressure from a strong lobby in government that included his defence minister, **Shimon Peres**, and members of the National Religious Party (NRP), who favoured settlement building in highly populated areas of the West Bank. Rabin was totally opposed to this, fearing that it would undermine his strategy for negotiating an agreement with Jordan over the area's future.

The Gush Emunim Settler Movement

In Rabin's first year as prime minister, the settler movement **Gush Emunim** emerged as the spearhead of a national campaign to return the whole of *Eretz* Israel to Jewish sovereignty. Its followers promoted the settlement of Samaria and Judea, the biblical names given by most Israelis to the northern and

Members of Gush Emunim establish a new settlement.

southern halves of the West Bank, respectively. They saw settling the Land of Israel as a religious obligation, a response to divine commandment. A minority within government, especially in the NRP, shared this messianic vision, which saw in Jewish settlement the way to redemption.

Gush Emunim appeared to some Israelis as the "new pioneers," a new sabra generation, and they converted public figures, from poets to politicians, to their cause.[8] In the climate of confusion and bewilderment that followed the Yom Kippur War of 1973, when the Israelis had been caught by surprise and sustained considerable losses, the Gush Emunim settlers stood for conviction and commitment. They created a nationalist fervor that swayed successive, wavering cabinets. And, in Ariel Sharon, former army general, the settlers' champion and now a special adviser to the prime minister, they had support at the heart of government.

In 1975, Gush Emunim activists settled in Sebastia, a village in the densely populated, mountainous area of the West Bank where the government had so far prevented settlement building. The activists were evacuated by soldiers, but they returned. This happened several times, accompanied by great publicity. Eventually, Defense Minister Peres and Sharon brokered a compromise that allowed thirty settlers to stay at a nearby military camp, later becoming the settlement of Kdumim.

The settlement of Ofra was founded in the same year. It had been designated as an army base, and a "work brigade" of settlers offered to build a fence for a private contractor constructing an army camp nearby. The army refused to let the settlers stay overnight but were overridden by Peres. Later, Peres ordered the army to provide an electricity generator for the settlers. Their families joined them, and their camp gradually evolved into a permanent settlement.

In similar ways, Gush Emunim settled further sites without government permission, intending to elicit legitimacy retroactively. The government did appear to oppose the activities of "rogue elements" and broke up some attempts at settlement building. Yet at its center were politicians for whom the settlers were a useful means for promoting a deliberate policy of settlement building.

Settlement Building under the Likud Government
The pace of settlement building intensified when a Likud government, led by Menachem Begin, came to power in 1977 and ended thirty years of Labor-led government. Its success was based on its support from the Mizrahim, the Jews who had immigrated to Israel from Arab lands, many of whom resented the domination of the European Ashkenazi Jews and their descendants. The Mizrahi Jews now made up nearly 50 percent of Jewish Israelis.

The new prime minister was a champion of Greater Israel, a Jewish state in all the land between the Mediterranean and the Jordan River. He appointed Ariel Sharon as head of the government's Ministerial Settlement Committee. The "Sharon Plan" called for settlement in the western highlands of the West Bank to take control of the most significant Palestinian agricultural land and more water resources.

Yet again, there was conflict and confusion in the Israeli government: some ministers argued settlement building in densely populated Arab areas was likely to provoke conflict and was therefore a threat to Israel's security. This probably explains why Sharon confused both his cabinet colleagues and opponents with his changing plans and talk of "archaeological sites," "workers' camps," and "military bases," which were, in effect, new settlements. The resulting chaos created a climate that allowed the illegal activity to continue. The government could, and did, disclaim responsibility for the actions of militant settlers, disowning their activities in the court of international opinion, all while supporting the ideological objective of a Greater Israel, which most of them shared.

Not all settlements were inhabited by ideologically driven men and women. Situated on the eastern outskirts of Jerusalem, Ma'ale Adumim was originally built to "strengthen Israel's grip on Jerusalem."[9] Ariel Sharon oversaw its transformation into the largest urban settlement in the West Bank.

It was located where the settlers and the army could control the major routes from Jerusalem to Jericho and the Dead Sea. It therefore fit the Likud strategy of capturing ground and extending Israeli control further inside the West Bank. Now, with a new highway constructed to connect it to Jerusalem, most of its inhabitants were attracted from the city by good, cheap housing, low taxes, or financial grants. Many of them commuted by day to Jerusalem or Tel Aviv.

Meanwhile, Gush Emunim settlers established outposts, often on high ground with a commanding position that overlooked Arab villages, with or without initial government support. They often provoked clashes with the local inhabitants. This sometimes suited the government because the resulting instability was construed as a threat to Israeli security, therefore justifying, under the Hague Convention, settlement on a "temporary" basis.[10] Further instability as a result could then act as further evidence that the settlement's continued existence was necessary. The settlers were often armed by the military and authorised to arrest Palestinians of whom they were suspicious.

In many different ways, the Israeli state, through the military and settlements, came to control much of the West Bank and Gaza. By 1987, twenty years after the occupation began, about 40 percent of Palestinian land in the West Bank had been confiscated by Israel and over fifty thousand Jews had moved there. About a third of Gaza had been taken over.

Not only did the Israelis control much of the land and its resources, but many of them also believed that the occupation was "enlightened." Literacy rates and healthcare had improved under Israeli administration, and employment in Israel enabled many Palestinians to sustain their families living in the West Bank and in Gaza. By 1985, a hundred thousand Palestinians were crossing into Israel daily to work in agriculture, construction, and a variety of menial jobs. Although usually lower than that of the Israelis, their wages were higher than they were likely to command in the occupied territories, where economic opportunities were far fewer.

Nevertheless, the Palestinian experience of life under occupation led to the eruption of the First Intifada, or uprising, in December 1987. This was to dramatically engulf the occupied territories.

Personal Testimony

David Grossman

David Grossman is an Israeli writer who spent several weeks in the West Bank in early 1987, talking to both Israelis and Palestinians. He visited the Palestinian refugee camp of Dheisheh, in Bethlehem. It is one of several such camps that were set up in the West Bank after 1948. He talked to the teachers and children in the kindergarten:

"The children here know everything. Some of the children here are the fourth generation on the camp. On any night the army may enter their house, right into the house, conduct a search, shout, turn over blankets and slash at them with their bayonets, strip their fathers – here, Naji here –"

Naji is two and a half years old, short for his age, black eyes, curls. "A month ago, they took his father, and he doesn't know where he is, or if he will ever return."

"A little while ago," says the second teacher, "the military governor visited the kindergarten and asked if I teach the children bad things, against Israel and the Jews."

"And what did you say to him?"

"I said that I don't. But that his soldiers do."

"What do soldiers do?" I ask a girl of about four, called Naima, green-eyed, little gold earrings in her ears.

"Searches and beatings."

"Do you know who the Jews are?"

"The army."

"What does your father do?"

"Sick."

"And your mother?"

"She works in Jerusalem for the Jews. Cleans their houses."

"And you" – a chubby boy, somewhat dreamy – "do you know who the Jews are?"

"Yes. They took my sister."

"Where to?"

"To Farah."

(Both his sisters are there, in jail, the teachers explain.)

"They did *not* throw stones," he says angrily.

Suddenly a little boy gets up, holding a short yellow plastic stick in his hand, and shoots me.

"Why are you shooting me?" He is two years old.

"Who do you want to shoot?" the teachers ask, smiling, like two mothers taking pride in a smart child.

"Jews."

"Now tell him why," they encourage the little one.

"Because the Jews took my uncle," he says. "At night, they came in and stole him from the bed, so now I sleep with my mother all the time."

It doesn't matter at all who is really guilty of the refugee camps. It is us [the Israelis] they

will hate, these children living their whole
lives in a colorless world without happiness,
who spend long summer and winter hours in
a cold and mildewed kindergarten, which has
neither a glass window nor electricity.[11]

Grossman spent a weekend in Ofra, an Israeli settlement founded by Gush Emunim followers in 1975.
He held a meeting with a group of residents, some
of whom were:

... members of the Jewish terrorist underground, arrested three years ago. Its members
were convicted variously of booby-trapping
the cars of the mayors of four West Bank cities,
of killing two students, of planting bombs in
Arab buses and of conspiring to blow up the
Dome of the Rock, the Moslem shrine which
sits on the site of the ancient Jewish Temple.

I told of my meetings with Arabs in the
area, of the pent-up hatred I found among
some of them; I told them of my visits to
the refugee camps ... I asked for their good
will. For their cooperation in one matter that
bothers me. Because I am very curious to see
if they can imagine themselves in their Arab
neighbours' places and tell me what seems to
them to be the most hateful manifestation of
the occupation.

Someone said immediately, "The situation
isn't our fault!" And others murmured their
agreement. I said: "That is not the question.

Let's assume you are right. I ask only for a little flexibility. What, in your opinions, does an Arab in his everyday life, in his most private meditations, in his relations with his children, in what does he most feel the influence of your (just, you believe) presence here, in a place he sees as his land?"

"We haven't taken one meter of land from the Arabs," one woman said heatedly.

The people in the room were not able, even for a little while, to shift their point of view; they did not allow themselves even a split second of empathy and uncommitted participation in the lives of those whose fates are intertwined and interwoven so much with theirs. Like fossils, they did not succeed in freeing themselves from those very bonds which they are unwilling to admit exist.

Then Yehuda said that the answer is simple: that he does not want to think even for a minute about the situation of the Arabs around him, because he is caught up in a struggle with them, at war, he said, and were he to allow himself to pity, to identify, he would weaken and endanger himself. The people in the room nodded.

Theirs is a closed society with a clear internal code of its own, of people with, in general, very similar biographies, interacting with each other over a course of years, people who have been moulded since childhood by the same common experiences and struggles. [They have a] "bunker mentality," and it is hard to know whether they hate this or whether it is essential to their continued survival and faith.

The members of Gush Emunim have created their own prison, out of which they peek, stiff and prickly, in the face of all other opinions ... They see the Bible as an operational order. An operation that, even if its time has yet to come, will come and, if it does not come soon enough, will need to be brought. I fear life among a people who have an obligation to an absolute order. Absolute orders require, in the end, absolute deeds and I am a partial, relative, imperfect man who prefers to make correctible mistakes rather than attain supernatural achievements.[12]

CHAPTER 7

Palestinian Resistance and the First Intifada
1967–87

This chapter explains how Palestinian resistance developed after 1967 and then examines the uprising which became known as the First Intifada.

- Why was the Six-Day War a turning point for the PLO?
- What impact did the PLO have on the Israeli-Palestinian conflict after 1967?
- Why were the PLO and Israelis in Lebanon?
- What was the First Intifada and how was it sustained?

Fatah and the PLO

During and immediately after the Six-Day War of 1967, over 250,000 Palestinians fled from the West Bank and Gaza when the territories were captured by the Israelis. Most went to Jordan. The majority of them were refugees of the first Arab-Israeli War of 1948–49, and now they were refugees a second time.

For the million or more who remained in the West Bank and Gaza, resistance to Israeli military occupation was harshly dealt with and interpreted very broadly: holding a rally or demonstration, organizing a strike, distributing a leaflet, or just waving the Palestinian flag. The movement of Palestinians was closely monitored, and they were regularly

The Israeli conquest of the West Bank in 1967 drove more than 250,000 Palestinians across the Jordan River over the Allenby Bridge, which was destroyed in the Six-Day War.

stopped at roadblocks. Israeli troops rounded up PLO suspects and others whom they saw as a threat to their security. Thousands were jailed; some were tortured or had their houses blown up, leaving their families homeless. Hundreds were deported (usually to Jordan), and in Gaza, tens of thousands were forced to leave.

The refugee camps, particularly in Jordan, were swollen by new waves of Palestinians displaced during and after the war. In fact, by 1967, half the population of Jordan was Palestinian. Fatah and other groups now concentrated their forces in Jordan and started to recruit far more volunteers from the refugee camps.

Many Palestinians were now convinced that they would have to fight for their homeland on their own. This was particularly important now that the frontline states of Egypt and Syria were preoccupied with the recovery of the land they had lost to Israel in the Six-Day War (the Sinai and the Golan Heights, respectively – see map on p. 106) while King Hussein of Jordan was widely blamed for "losing" the rest of Palestine. The liberation of Palestine was even more urgent now that all the original land of Palestine, including the West Bank and Gaza Strip, was under Israeli rule.

Fatah, the largest Palestinian resistance group, now took the initiative. Its leadership was emboldened by the growth in recruitment to its ranks and the development of its training facilities, particularly in refugee camps in Syria and Jordan. Ghazi Daniel was one of those who joined Fatah in the aftermath of the Six-Day War:

> The aggressive war of 1967 was a landmark in my life. The new expansion of Israel and the new waves of refugees multiplied the tragedy many times ... I am left with no alternative but to fight our oppressor. This is why I have joined the Palestine National Liberation Movement. We shall fight for the Palestinians' return and for a new society in Palestine.[1]

Yasser Arafat, the Fatah leader, persuaded his colleagues that now was the time to launch the armed struggle from within the Israeli-occupied territories. He was convinced that it would boost morale and encourage Palestinians in those territories to remain on their lands. Encouraged by signs of civilian resistance (in the form of strikes and sit-ins, for example), Arafat insisted that Fatah was now ready to move to a "popular liberation war."[2] Guerrilla commanders were sent into the

West Bank to encourage continuing resistance to Israeli military rule and to provide basic military training for the inhabitants. Military operations were started in late August 1967.

The result was a failure. Fatah operations were poorly organised. They did not yet have a strong enough network of support in the territories and there was little sign of mass participation. It was too soon to launch a popular liberation war.

Israeli countermeasures were swift and effective. Curfews were imposed in villages suspected of supporting Fatah, the houses of suspected militants were demolished, and thousands were arrested. Fatah security was lax, and by using informers, the Israelis were able to infiltrate their forces. By the end of 1967, two hundred Fatah guerrillas had been killed and a thousand captured.[3] Arafat was forced to withdraw his remaining fighters to Jordan.

Yet, out of defeat, Fatah could point to significant achievement. Fatah had shown willingness to avenge the Arab defeat in the Six-Day War. Talk of coexistence with the occupying Israeli forces in the West Bank and Gaza was stifled. Fatah attracted many more recruits, and the flow of funds from Arab countries increased. Several Palestinian guerrilla groups benefited, but it was Fatah that emerged as the strongest.

Fatah established military bases in Jordan, the country that had the largest number of refugees and the longest border with Israel and the West Bank. Privately, the Jordanian King Hussein was opposed to this military buildup and the effects of Israeli retaliation that met each attack on Israel. However, there was huge popular support for the Fatah guerrillas, and publicly the government welcomed their actions. In the first three months of 1968, Fatah carried out seventy- eight attacks on Israeli targets.

The "Battle of Karameh"

Then, on March 21, 1968, Fatah achieved a remarkable breakthrough. In mid-March, Israel planned a major attack on Fatah bases in and around the village of Karameh, four miles inside Jordan. Jordanian intelligence got wind of the plan and advised the Palestinian fighters to withdraw. Fatah's leaders, however, decided to stay and fight.

Backed by tanks and aircraft, an Israeli force of fifteen thousand attacked. In the ensuing battle, Fatah lost ninety-two of its three hundred men and Israel largely destroyed the Fatah bases. However, in the words of the historian Yezid Sayigh, "the battle of Karameh turned overnight into a resounding political and psychological victory in Arab eyes."[4]

Against overwhelming odds, Fatah's fighters had stood their ground, something that the three regular Arab armies of Egypt, Syria, and Jordan had been unable to do in June 1967. Furthermore, twenty-eight Israeli soldiers were killed and several Israeli tanks destroyed. Fatah's fighters, backed by Jordanian forces, had proved that the Israelis were not invincible, and Karameh was portrayed as a heroic triumph.

The word *karameh* means "honor" or "dignity" in Arabic, and the news of the Battle of Karameh spread. It was as if the honor of all Arabs had been defended. Five thousand joined Fatah in the following two days. In the eyes of most Palestinians, Fatah was now *the* Palestinian movement.

At this time, the image of the Palestinian fighter wearing the **keffiyeh**, the traditional peasant headdress, with gun in hand, became synonymous with the cause of Palestine. No longer powerless refugees but empowered fighters, the guerrillas were portrayed similarly to the youth of the sabra generation of Zionists in the 1930s (see p. 32) – bold, brave, full of pride, and committed to their people's national cause. Fatah and other groups also started programs to improve conditions in the camps, setting up their own educational and medical facilities.

The Fatah leadership, now confident of its own position in the vanguard of popular, armed resistance to Israel, believed it

A Palestinian fighter wearing a *keffiyeh*

had the experience to fuse all the different guerrilla groups together under its control. Within a year of the Battle of Karameh, Fatah gained control of the PLO and, in 1969, Yasser Arafat became its chairman. The new Charter of the PLO proclaimed, "Armed struggle is the only way to liberate Palestine."

Terrorism and the Palestinian Struggle

Arafat tried to coordinate the guerrilla activities of the various groups that came under the umbrella of the PLO. Like most of the PLO leaders, he wanted to limit the raids and the bombings to Israeli territory and targets because he believed the Palestinians' military aim should be strictly focused on war on Israel. However, more radical Palestinian groups, such as the Popular Front for the Liberation of Palestine (PFLP), started to carry out attacks in other parts of the world. They pointed out that raids into Israel had achieved very little. They were impatient. They were not prepared to wait ten or twenty years to regain their country.

In December 1968, two members of the PFLP hijacked an Israeli passenger plane at Athens Airport, killing one man. The Israelis retaliated by destroying thirteen aircraft in an attack on Beirut Airport in Lebanon, from where the hijackers had flown. In the following years, there were many hijackings, kidnappings, and bombings in Europe and elsewhere. At first the targets were Israeli planes, embassies, and offices, but in February 1970 a Swiss plane was blown up on its way to Israel.

Palestinian militants referred to these attacks as "external operations," although in the West they were seen as acts of terrorism. George Habash, the leader of the PFLP, explained:

> When we hijack a plane it has more effect than if we killed 100 Israelis in battle. For decades world public opinion has been neither for nor against the Palestinians. It simply ignored us. At least the world is talking about us now.[5]

The Israelis usually responded to these attacks by bombing Palestinian bases in Lebanon, Jordan, and Syria. Often these bases were near refugee camps and, as a consequence, hundreds of innocent Palestinians died. Israeli reprisals received far less publicity in the Western press than the Palestinian attacks. Nevertheless, many Palestinians remained defiant, like this mother when interviewed:

> I am proud that my son did not die in this refugee camp. The foreign press come here and take pictures of us standing in queues to obtain food rations. This is no life. I am proud that my son died in action, fighting on our occupied soil. I am already preparing my eight-year-old for the day he can fight for freedom too.[6]

Sometimes terrorist violence led Arab to fight Arab. In Jordan, the PLO were acting as if they ruled much of the country, not just the refugee camps. They roamed fully armed and set up roadblocks,

A British plane blown up in Jordan

even in Amman, the Jordanian capital. Moreover, King Hussein feared the Israeli reprisals that followed Palestinian attacks launched from his country. In September 1970, he decided there would be no more such attacks. He ordered the Palestinians to obey him and his army.

Then, in the same month, four aircraft were hijacked by the PFLP and three of the planes (belonging to British Airways, Swissair, and TWA) were taken to an airfield in Jordan. The hijackers demanded the release of Palestinian fighters jailed in Britain, Germany, Switzerland, and Israel. The passengers were set free and then the planes were blown up.

This incident was the last straw for King Hussein. It was a direct challenge to his authority, and he feared further foreign intervention. He ordered his army to take control of the PLO bases. The Palestinians resisted, and in the next ten days more than three thousand of them were killed by Jordanian forces. Egyptian President Nasser played a key role in arranging a ceasefire, but over the following nine months the last Palestinian military bases in Jordan were eliminated and the remaining fighters were expelled, most moving to Syria and Lebanon.

In revenge, the Jordanian prime minister was murdered while he was in Egypt. The killers were members of a group called Black September, named after the month in which the

Palestinian bases in Jordan were wiped out. Two years later, on September 5, 1972, members of Black September captured eleven Israeli athletes competing in the Olympic Games in Munich, West Germany. They killed two of the athletes and then demanded the release of two hundred Palestinians in prison in Israel. When police attempted a rescue, the Palestinians killed the remaining nine athletes.

The Palestinians received the massive publicity they wanted for their cause but not the release of their comrades. A few days later, the Israelis carried out reprisal raids on PLO bases in Syria and Lebanon, in which over two hundred people were killed.

Across the world, people were shocked by the group's brutal deeds. They branded the PLO as terrorists. However, many people in Europe and other parts of the world began to think more about the Palestinian problem. They read about the crowded, unhealthy camps in which hundreds of thousands of refugees had lived for over twenty years. With growing understanding in the West of the plight of the Palestinians, some politicians came to see that Yasser Arafat was, in the words of the French foreign minister, a "moderate" who "represents and embodies the aspirations of the Palestinians." In November 1974, Arafat was invited to address a full meeting of the United Nations.

Arafat at the United Nations, 1974

Arafat and other moderate PLO leaders had hinted that they were ready to consider a "mini-state," consisting of the West Bank and Gaza, for the Palestinians. In other words, they were no longer determined to destroy the State of Israel. Arafat now acknowledged that Israel, with the full support of the United States and the recognition of nearly all the international community, was here to stay.

Although some Western states were still very skeptical, the UN representatives of the Soviet Union and its allies, together with those of many Asian and African countries, combined to secure an invitation for Arafat to speak at the United Nations. Before dawn on November 13, 1974, he was flown by US helicopter to the UN building in New York amid the tightest security in the organisation's history. He gave his speech with a holster attached to his hip, although he had left his gun outside:

> The roots of the Palestinian question are not the result of a conflict between two religions or two national-isms. Neither is it a border conflict between two neighboring states. It is the cause of a people deprived of its homeland, dispersed and uprooted, and living mostly in exile and in refugee camps. . . . Today I have come bearing an olive branch and a freedom fighter's gun. Do not let the olive branch fall from my hand.[7]

Many of his listeners were sympathetic to his message: that the Palestinian problem was about a people who had been forced to flee from their homes and who were still, after twenty-five years, living in refugee camps. Some world leaders were beginning to admit that the Palestinians deserved a homeland. They also believed that if the Palestinians were granted their wish, permanent peace in the Middle East would be possible.

Although Arafat received a sympathetic hearing at the United Nations, there was no breakthrough to peace. The Israelis were furious with the United Nations for inviting Arafat to speak. They said the PLO was a "murder organi-sation." They refused to discuss the idea of a separate Pales-tinian state, however small it might be. They feared that the

Palestinians aimed to take back all of Israel and would not be content with a small state next door.

The PLO was itself divided. Some hardliners still insisted that Israel should be destroyed and taken over by Palestinians. They rejected the idea of a Palestinian "mini-state" and did not want any Arab state to recognise Israel.

The PLO in Lebanon

Lebanon was a fairly stable country until the 1970s. Its capital, Beirut, was one of the richest cities in the Middle East. Most of the population were either Christian or Muslim, although both groups were made up of several different sects. Since 1943, they had kept to an agreement that the president would be a Christian and the prime minister a Muslim, and that just over half the posts in government would go to the Christian majority. However, by the 1970s, the Muslims outnumbered the Christians and were demanding more power.

Many Palestinians had come to Lebanon as refugees in 1948–49 and more arrived after the Six-Day War of 1967. By 1970, there were about a quarter of a million in Lebanon. However, the most destabilizing force in Lebanon was the PLO, whose armed forces had set up bases after they were expelled from Jordan in 1970. Soon they came to dominate southern Lebanon, which some Israelis dubbed "Fatahland."

In the refugee camps, the PLO established courts, imposed taxes, and provided military training for the young men. They also provided a basic system of social welfare: the Palestinian Red Crescent Society, of which Yasser Arafat's brother was the chairman, built ten hospitals and many clinics by the early 1980s. They set up a radio network and several newspapers. With financial aid from the oil-rich Arab states in the Gulf, the PLO built up a bureaucracy, employing about eight thousand civil servants and creating the infrastructure of a state in the making.

The PLO also launched new attacks on Israel, particularly on villages in the Galilee region in the north. When the Israelis hit back, those killed became heroes in the camps, "martyrs" whose faces appeared on posters on walls and whose families received special pensions.

However, Lebanese people were also killed when the Israelis retaliated, and in 1975, Lebanon's largely Christian military forces tried to regain control of the south of the country. The Palestinians resisted and were helped by Lebanese Muslims. Soon, Lebanon was caught up in a civil war that was mainly between Christians and Muslims. Meanwhile, the PLO continued to carry out attacks on Israel. In 1978, a PLO suicide squad went further south and attacked a bus near Tel Aviv, killing thirty-seven passengers.

Three days after the bus bombing, Israeli troops invaded Lebanon. They seized the south of the country, but the PLO forces melted away. The Israelis withdrew under pressure from the United States, and United Nations troops were sent to keep the peace on the Lebanese-Israeli border.

Over the next four years, the Palestinian armed forces grew in strength. Lebanon had become the focus of their military operations against Israel, and they received a constant stream of recruits from the Palestinians in the refugee camps in Lebanon.

The Israeli Invasion of Lebanon, 1982

In the early months of 1982, the Israeli leaders, Prime Minister Begin and Defense Minister Sharon, planned another invasion of Lebanon. They saw it as a "war for the Land of Israel," believing that, if Israel destroyed the PLO's independent power base in Lebanon, then Palestinian resistance in the West Bank and Gaza would wither away.

The Israelis simply needed a pretext. It came in June 1982 when a group of Palestinians opposed to Yasser Arafat attempted to murder the Israeli ambassador in London. This was the justification the Israelis needed, and their forces again crossed the Lebanese border. This time, they had eighty thousand troops and nearly a thousand tanks. The UN peacekeeping forces were powerless to stop them.

The Israelis were more successful in destroying PLO forces than they had been in 1978. However, thousands of Palestinian and Lebanese civilians were killed in the process and hundreds of thousands were made homeless.

Begin and Sharon had led the Israeli Cabinet to believe that the aim was to drive out the Palestinian forces, destroy their bases, and establish a twenty-five-mile security zone in southern Lebanon to protect the Israelis living in Galilee. However, it soon became obvious that Sharon was far more ambitious as the Israelis advanced north and surrounded Beirut. They cut off supplies of food and water and started shelling positions held by the PLO. Such positions were often in crowded residential areas so thousands more civilians were killed.

As well as encircling Beirut on land, the Israelis had complete control of the sky and the coastline. Beirut was bombarded daily, from air, land, and sea, for two months. On one day alone in August 1982, 127 air raids were launched on the city. Over twenty thousand were killed and many more wounded during the "Battle of Beirut."

Lebanese politicians pressed the PLO to leave. Then, in mid-August, the United States intervened. It persuaded the Israelis to stop shelling the city in return for an agreement that the PLO fighters would be evacuated. American, French, and Italian troops were sent to supervise the evacuation. Over fourteen thousand Palestinian fighters left Beirut to travel to other Arab states. Yasser Arafat, the last to leave, moved his headquarters to Tunisia.

The Americans had assured Arafat that Palestinian civilians would not be harmed after the PLO forces left Beirut. However, the Israelis believed that there were still two thousand Palestinian fighters left in the refugee camps of Sabra and Shatila in West Beirut.

When, on September 14, the newly elected Christian president of Lebanon was killed, his armed supporters took their revenge by invading the refugee camps and, over the next two days, carried out a massacre of Palestinian men, women, and children. The Israeli troops were ordered by their officers to let them in and not to intervene. They stood by. Investigators later reckoned that between one thousand and two thousand were killed.

In Israel, a crowd of four hundred thousand led by members of the recently formed **Peace Now** movement protested

Israeli opponents of the war in Lebanon, 1982

against the actions of their armed forces. An Israeli government inquiry later found Sharon indirectly responsible for the massacre and said he was unfit to be defence minister. He was forced to resign.

After the PLO forces left Beirut, the Israelis withdrew their troops from the city. However, they remained in the south of Lebanon. They had succeeded in driving out the Palestinian armed forces but could not be sure that they had driven *all* of them out: the guerrillas could easily hide in the huge, crowded refugee camps in southern Lebanon. And the Israelis had made many enemies among the Lebanese, especially the Muslims in the south. Many of these were to become members of Hezbollah, a fiercely anti-Israeli organisation.

Over the next two years, Israeli troops in the south of Lebanon were regularly attacked, and an increasing number of Israeli citizens demanded a complete withdrawal from Lebanon. In 1985, Israeli troops withdrew from most of Lebanon, leaving only a small military presence in the "security zone" along the southern border. This was the longest war Israel had fought. Many regarded it as its first defeat.

The Israeli government may have been confident that it had destroyed the PLO's independent base in Lebanon and brought about the eviction of its fighters from the country. However, Palestinian resistance was far from over.

The First Intifada, 1987–93

On December 8, 1987, an Israeli Army vehicle in the Jabalya refugee camp in Gaza crashed into two cars, killing four Palestinians. Rumors spread that it had been a deliberate act of revenge for the killing of an Israeli settler two days before.

The funerals of the Palestinians became huge demonstrations. At one of them a youth was shot dead by an Israeli soldier, and in retaliation, a nearby Israeli Army post was attacked. Thousands took to the streets and alleyways of the camp. They put up barricades of tires and corrugated iron and stoned Israeli Army patrols.

The demonstrations spread across Gaza and the West Bank. Soon the First Intifada (literally, "shaking off"), as the uprising came to be known, involved children and adults, women and men, labourers and businessmen, villagers and townspeople. What started as a spontaneous, unplanned action became a national uprising. The intifada may have been triggered by a single incident, but why did such a wide-spread rebellion erupt at this time?

The daily humiliations of life under occupation had been accumulating for some time and, by 1984, nearly 250,000 Palestinians (10 percent of the entire population of the occupied territories) had experienced detention or interrogation by Israeli military forces. However, the oppressive nature of Israeli rule became even more intense in the years from 1984 to 1987.

The pace of land confiscation and settlement building increased, with seventeen new settlements created in those three years, several of them in areas that were densely populated by Palestinians. Violence increased, with more attacks on the Israeli military and, in response, the Israeli government adopted an "iron fist" policy of more arrests, beatings, imprisonment without trial, house demolitions, and deportations.

Curfews were extended and some schools and universities, seen as centers of resistance, were closed. Palestinian workers who migrated daily to Israel continued to face discrimination in pay and working conditions and suffered mistreatment by their Israeli employers. Meanwhile, money sent home to their families by Palestinians working in the rich Gulf states diminished as the oil economy slowed down. With unemployment increasing (it was 35 percent in the refugee camps of Gaza) and little economic hope for the future, many, especially among the younger generations, felt they had nothing to lose from breaking loose.

Sustaining the Intifada

Young people, often teenagers, were foremost in the demonstrations. With nothing more than stones and catapults, they skirmished with Israeli military patrols. The "children of the stones," wearing their keffiyehs as masks, became the symbols of the intifada (see image on p. 133). And the adults backed them up, passing on word from local activists about where the next demonstration would be held.

"Popular committees," informal grassroots organisations, were set up to sustain the uprising. Often, they were based on groups – for students, workers, women, or professionals – that had been formed under the aegis of the PLO in previous years.

Stone-throwing youths confronting heavily armed Israeli troops became familiar images during the First Intifada, generating much sympathy for the Palestinians worldwide.

Action was taken locally. Women came forward, organizing classes when schools were shut down and establishing welfare services for the families of a *shahid*, or martyr, killed by the troops. When boycotts of Israeli goods were called for, "merchants committees" enforced them.

In January 1988, the **Unified National Leadership of the Uprising (UNLU)** emerged to coordinate the strikes and demonstrations. Its leaders largely remained unknown, deliberately so, to avoid arrest, but its clandestine leaflets were widely distributed. Writing of Ramallah, the West Bank town where she lived, Penny Johnson recorded:

> People look down to spot the latest statement from the Unified Leadership of the Uprising, often found in the street or tucked under a windshield or door. For the first time in many years, words have a direct bearing on individual or collective action. People shape their daily lives around the announcements of general strikes, demonstrations from churches or mosques, and "assignments" to different sectors of the population.[8]

The first UNLU leaflet called for a general strike, urging Palestinians to resign from their jobs working for the Israelis, whether in the settlements or the Israeli administration in the occupied territories. Warnings against strike breaking were issued and most took heed. The UNLU leadership sought the approval of the PLO for their leaflets, but the initiative was taken locally and there was widespread agreement throughout the Palestinian community on the decision not to take up arms.

Whole communities were mobilised, with most people accepting the authority of the "popular committees." Israeli goods were shunned and "agricultural committees" were formed to help grow more local produce. The Palestinian economy became much more self-sufficient, and the Israeli economy suffered accordingly. However, as the number of Palestinians working by day in Israel dropped dramatically, so did the standard of living in the territories. This was especially the case in the latter stages of the intifada when the Israelis cut off vital supplies of gasoline, electricity, and water.

The First Intifada bore close similarities to the Revolt of 1936–39. Both uprisings had taken the leadership by surprise – the "notables" in 1936 and the Tunis-based PLO in 1987. Although the AHC in 1936 and UNLU in 1988 were set up to coordinate and direct the rebellions, it was local groups who sustained them.

Rural Palestine played a major part in both: in the intifada, many villages declared themselves "liberated" and flew the Palestinian flag. As in the 1930s, the villagers were often met with house demolitions, mass beatings, and arrests of the menfolk by the Israeli forces. Those suspected of collaborating with the Israelis were harshly dealt with, and as in the 1930s, hundreds of them were killed by other Palestinians.

The Israeli Response

From the start of the First Intifada, the Israeli government intensified their "iron fist" policy: their troops used tear gas, water cannons, rubber bullets, and even live ammunition. But they could not halt the momentum of the uprising.

Newspapers and television around the world showed teenagers being shot by Israeli troops. This led the Israeli government to announce that it would no longer use bullets. Instead, they adopted a policy of "might, force and beatings." There were mass arrests and increased use of "harsh interrogation" (torture) and special detention camps were set up. Defense Minister Rabin was heard talking of the need to "break [the rioters'] bones."[9]

Many of those thought to be leading the uprising were held in administrative detention (without trial), as were women and children as young as fourteen. But there was no end to the intifada and the death rate kept rising. By September 1988, 346 Palestinians had been killed. Many of them were under the age of sixteen.

The Palestinians knew that they could not defeat the Israelis militarily, but they could force them to acknowledge that the occupation was not sustainable, and they could arouse international opinion to put pressure on Israel. Beatings and other punishments meted out to men, women, and children were shown on television screens around the world; and the public, in Israel and abroad, was made increasingly aware of the coercive nature of the occupation.

The world saw a powerful, modern army let loose against civilians fighting for their human rights and the right to self-governance. Over a thousand Palestinians were killed by Israeli troops during the years of the First Intifada, from 1987 to 1993, and 175,000 were imprisoned at one time or another (180 Israelis were killed, both civilians and security personnel). A nighttime curfew was imposed, and the widespread closure of schools and universities was imposed. Birzeit University, the foremost university in the West Bank, was closed for four years.

Some Israelis demanded even harsher treatment of the Palestinians, including mass deportation ("transfer"), to end the intifada. However, many Israelis came to see that the intifada was a genuinely popular rising that could not be put down by military means. Some of them argued that there had to be a political solution. Many Palestinians in Gaza and the West Bank came to the same conclusion.

The intifada undoubtedly increased and strengthened the sense of community and nationhood among the Palestinians, but it did not improve their miserable living conditions nor end the occupation. Palestinian leaders in the occupied territories realised they had to put pressure on the PLO leadership in Tunisia to seek a political solution, to recognise Israel and acknowledge that they, the Palestinians, would never be able liberate the whole of Palestine.

In November 1988, the PLO issued a Declaration of Independence, proclaiming "the establishment of the State of Palestine" alongside Israel. Arafat recognised Israel's right to exist and signaled the end of the "armed struggle." At the time, the two announcements were largely drowned out by the noise of events on the ground, but they led the US government to open discussions with PLO representatives, which it had hitherto refused to do.

The First Intifada, and Israel's response to it, exposed the failure of Israel's methods of controlling the civilian population of the West Bank and Gaza. Israeli policy was now revealed, to most Israelis, as too economically, politically, and morally expensive.

The deployment of huge numbers of troops imposed a considerable financial burden on Israel and it was politically divisive. Above all, the occupation was exposed, in the words of the Israeli political scientist Neve Gordon, "for what it was – that is, military rule upheld through violence and violation."[10]

This view of Israeli policy came to be shared widely in the international community. An alternative way of maintaining Israel's hold on the West Bank and Gaza, one that was not so dependent on military force, would have to be found. The road to Oslo and the "peace process" is explained in the next chapter.

Personal Testimony
Remembering the First Intifada

Khaled Ziadeh was seventeen years old when the intifada started. He was born in Gaza City but moved to Bureij refugee camp at the start of the uprising. The refugee camps in Gaza were centers of some of the most intense nationalist feeling and frequently the targets of Israeli fire power:

> We decided to protest and resist the military occupation with the little means we had. Markets, shops and schools stopped and crowds went on the streets in protest. Tear gas and the smoke of burning tires changed the color of the sky and all you heard was the sound of guns shooting live ammunition or rubber bullets that injured or killed. Taxis were used to carry the injured to local clinics. There were funerals almost every day.
>
> It was even during these conditions that a unified leadership emerged and factions came out of hiding to mobilise the population, and the intifada was a mixture of organised action and spontaneous acts of resistance.

The young people felt empowered and realised that history was on their side. Israel opened two new prisons, Ansar 2 and Ansar 3, to put behind bars the increasing number of detainees. Most of my friends were arrested more than once and it became clear that every young person knew he was waiting his turn to be incarcerated. The then Israeli Defense Minister Yitzhak Rabin issued an order to break the bones of young Palestinians. They did break bones and some days all you could see were people walking around in casts.

In the camp, a daily curfew was imposed for 12 hours a day, and sometimes, in response to protests and clashes, they would impose a curfew for a week or two to exhaust the people and sap their energy. Another form of collective punishment was that they would order everyone between the age of 16 and 50 to come out and make them sit from two till six in the morning in the cold. We paid a heavy price for the uprising: unemployment rose significantly and freedom of movement was restricted. Schools were out of bounds so we began informal education, at homes.

Everyone who lived and witnessed the *intifada* has a story to tell, some happy memories and some sad ones. It was wonderful to see the youth getting together and mobilizing to confront the army, and then hear them dancing the *dabke* [traditional Palestinian dance] in the streets and singing nationalist songs out in the open, unlike before when such activities were banned. Before the uprising, they banned performances of the *dabke* and you could receive a punishment of six months in prison if you defied this order.

For me, the *intifada* was when I began to feel what it means to be Palestinian. It is the same for all of my generation. You know, many Palestinians did not talk about the 1948 and 1967 defeats because they felt humiliated and ashamed. My grandfather did not talk about 1948 and all he talked about was the great life he lived before. My father always avoided speaking about the 1967 defeat. Both felt humiliated and ashamed. The first *intifada* changed all of that because there was something to talk about, and it was the beginning of a new generation of Palestinians that did not accept defeat.[11]

CHAPTER 8

The Rise and Demise of the Oslo Peace Process

1993–2000

In the 1990s, a remarkable breakthrough was made in peace-making between Israelis and Palestinians.

- **What led the Israelis and Palestinians to hold direct talks in the early 1990s?**
- **What were the Oslo Accords?**
- **What did they achieve?**
- **What went wrong?**

The handshake (see p. 153) was greeted with widespread applause, if not excitement, across the world in September 1993. It showed the accord between the Israeli leader Yitzhak Rabin, commander of Israeli troops in the Six-Day War and instigator of the "iron fist" policy in the occupied territories, and Yasser Arafat, whom he had previously denounced as leader of "a terrorist organisation." They had just signed a peace agreement that had been negotiated in Oslo, Norway. It was the most significant breakthrough in many years of attempted peacemaking between Israel and the Palestinians. Yet, by the year 2000, it had largely unraveled to become unworkable.

The Road to Oslo

By the early 1990s, Israelis as well as Palestinians were beginning to acknowledge that the First Intifada that had started

September 1993: After officially signing the first Oslo Accord, Israeli Prime Minister Yitzhak Rabin and PLO Chairman Yasser Arafat shake hands at a public ceremony in Washington DC, overseen by President Bill Clinton.

in 1987 was a war that could not be won by either side. There would have to be a change of strategy. Such a change, by both sides, was facilitated by the changing international context.

Following the disintegration of the Soviet Union in 1991, the US government proclaimed a "new world order." In the Middle East, the Americans were eager to maintain the support of Arab states that had backed their expulsion of Iraqi troops from Kuwait. They also wished to be seen as committed to the establishment of a wider peace in the Middle East and to ease their ally, Israel, out of the diplomatic isolation in which it found itself because of the First Intifada. A resolution of the Israel-Palestine conflict would serve all these purposes.

The Israelis and the US government were not the only ones who were eager to find a way out of the impasse. So, too, were the Palestinians. Both the "internal" leadership on the West Bank and in Gaza, and the PLO leaders, living in exile in Tunis, realised that only a negotiated settlement could resolve the continuing conflict.[1]

The Israelis knew that the PLO was diplomatically weak and financially drained. In 1990, when the Iraqi leader, Saddam Hussein, invaded Kuwait, a fellow Arab state, the PLO had declared its support for the invasion. It did so to show solidarity with the Iraqis, who had long supported the PLO. However, the result was the shunning of the PLO by most Arab states, as well as by the wider international community, and the withdrawal of financial support by the oil-rich Arab states in the Gulf. Moreover, the flow of remittances, from over two hundred thousand Palestinians working in Kuwait to their families back home in the occupied territories, dried up when most of the Palestinians were expelled.

Meanwhile, the PLO leadership in Tunisia was increasingly seen as out of touch by many Palestinians in the West Bank and Gaza. The PLO was also facing a challenge to its leadership of the Palestinian national movement from the rising influence of the Islamic Resistance Movement, best known as **Hamas**.

Founded in the occupied territories during the First Intifada, Hamas emerged as a political organisation out of the many Islamic charities that provided schools, medical clinics, and social welfare organisations in the occupied territories. Toward the end of the first year of the First Intifada, when the PLO had recognised Israel's right to exist and abandoned "armed struggle," Hamas resisted the move. Its leaders remained committed to the liberation of all of what had been British-controlled Palestine. The PLO, however, were more than ready for compromise with the Israelis by the early 1990s.

In October 1991, the US government put pressure on the Israeli leaders into holding talks with Palestinian leaders. The Israelis refused to meet the PLO but agreed to meet

Palestinians from the occupied territories. At the talks held in Madrid, the Palestinians spoke of the need for compromise, but the Israelis were intransigent and little progress was made. The United States, however, kept up the pressure on Israel and called on the Israelis to stop building more settlements in the occupied territories or risk losing their financial aid. Then, when elections were held in Israel in June 1992, a moderate Labour government, pledging to resolve the ongoing conflict in the occupied territories, was voted into power.

The new prime minister, Yitzhak Rabin, could see how desperate Arafat and the PLO leaders were to secure a foothold in the occupied territories. The PLO could fulfill the role of partner in agreeing to a "territorial compromise," on Israel's terms, something Rabin had long sought. As early as 1977, he had stated, "Certainly, if the PLO ceased to be the PLO, we would cease to consider it as such. Or if the tiger transformed itself into a horse, we could mount it."[2]

Both Rabin and his foreign minister, Shimon Peres, wanted a "land for peace" deal, exchanging land for peace to strengthen the security of the State of Israel. Such an agreement would also preserve Israel's Jewish and democratic nature. Formal annexation of the West Bank was ruled out because it would entail the incorporation of a large and fast-growing Palestinian population into the State of Israel and thus imperil its Jewish nature, while the Likud Party policy of "creeping annexation," without granting Israeli citizenship rights to Palestinians, harmed the democratic image of Israel.

Rabin and Peres were willing to negotiate a partial withdrawal from the main Palestinian cities, such as Ramallah, Bethlehem, and Hebron, while maintaining strategic domination of the occupied territories. They would do this through continued control of the Jordan Valley and East Jerusalem and its hinterland, together with the maintenance of the Israeli Army's responsibility for overall security of the West Bank. At the same time, they could delegate responsibility for day-to-day management of most of the Palestinian population to the PLO.

King Hussein had renounced any claim to the area at the start of the First Intifada and thus closed off the "Jordanian option" for managing the West Bank population. The "Palestinian option," in the form of a partnership with the PLO, was now a viable alternative.

Meanwhile, in August 1992, the US government revived talks between Israelis and Palestinians, the latter represented by "insiders" from the occupied territories. The main point of disagreement was the settlements: the Palestinians insisted on a complete halt to further building, to which the Israelis would not agree.

The Oslo Accords of 1993 and 1995

In January 1993 discussions were started between two different groups of Israelis and Palestinians. They were initiated by the Norwegian foreign minister and held in Oslo, the Norwegian capital, away from the glare of worldwide publicity. They were held in secret – not even the Israeli prime minister knew of them initially – and involved members of the PLO and two Israeli academics. Later, Israeli officials took over the Israeli side in the negotiations.

Finally, after eight months of talks, the Israeli prime minister and the chairman of the PLO shook hands after signing what became known as the **Oslo Accords**. The Accords consisted of two letters of mutual recognition and the Declaration of Principles. In the first of the two letters, Yasser Arafat recognised "the right of Israel to exist in peace and security," renounced the use of violence, and called for an end to the intifada. For his part, Yitzhak Rabin recognised "the PLO as the representative of the Palestinian people." Rabin's letter constituted a dramatic change in Israeli policy, but it did not do what the Palestinians most wanted. It did not recognise the Palestinians' right to national self-determination, let alone to a sovereign, independent state.

In the Declaration of Principles, Israel agreed to staged withdrawals of its forces from parts of the occupied territories, initially from Gaza and the West Bank city of Jericho, and the establishment of an elected **Palestinian Authority (PA)** in the territories. However, it represented an "interim" agreement in that the resolution of the core issues of the conflict – the status of Jerusalem, which Palestinians wanted as their capital, and Palestinian refugees, borders, and settlements – was postponed for future negotiations. These were to be completed within five years.

It was understood that peacemaking would be a gradual process, which would start with Israel giving up land and the Palestinians taking responsibility for law and order in the areas evacuated. It was envisaged that these small steps would enhance confidence and trust, thus creating a situation where the two sides could resolve the harder, "final status" issues over the next five years.

The letters and the Declaration were greeted with a wide degree of optimism among Israelis and Palestinians and in the wider world. Sari Nusseibeh, a Palestinian academic, expressed the joy shared by many Palestinians, "It meant no more harassment by soldiers, no more roadblocks, no more random arrests, no more land confiscation, no more settlement."[3]

Most Palestinians believed that the peace agreement was the first step toward the establishment of a Palestinian state and that the PA would lay the foundations for that new state. However, while Israel had achieved most of what it wanted – its right to security and its legitimacy recognised by the PLO – it made no commitment to the nature of any permanent peace settlement.

PLO leader Yasser Arafat waves to Palestinians on his way into Gaza, July 1994.

The Oslo II Accord, 1995

Two years later, in the so-called Oslo II Accord, it was agreed that elections to the PA would be held, several hundred Palestinian prisoners would be released in stages, and Israeli forces would be withdrawn from further Palestinian cities. The Accord also stipulated that the PA would be responsible for "combating terrorism and violence and preventing incitement to violence" in the territories.

In effect, the PLO, in the form of the PA, would act as Israel's partner in maintaining "public order." As Rabin said, the Palestinians would be responsible for security "in cooperation with Israel's security forces to safeguard Israel's security interests."[4] The PLO were transformed, in the words of Edward Said, a Palestinian American academic, into "Israel's enforcer."[5]

Most significant of all was the division of the West Bank into three areas, pending "permanent status negotiations." Area A was to include many Palestinian cities, which were to be "autonomous areas" and comprised 3 percent of the territory (see map on p. 159). Here, the PA had full responsibility for law and order. Area B, consisting of 23 percent of the territory, was to be policed by the PA but with the Israelis left in charge of overall security. Area C, making up

Areas A, B, and C of the West Bank, as agreed upon in Oslo II

74 percent of the territory, was to remain under the direct control of the Israeli military.

The PA was given responsibility for managing the needs of all the Palestinian population, but had full control of only 3 percent of the land – the seven biggest West Bank cities of Ramallah, Bethlehem, Nablus, Hebron, Jenin, Tulkarem, and Qalqilya. One of the chief benefits for Israel was that it was no longer responsible for the day-to-day control of most of the Palestinian population.

The PA was responsible not only for maintaining law and order in the main cities of Area A (and, partially, in Area B), but also for health, education, and welfare for Palestinians in all areas, relieving Israel of some of the most onerous aspects of occupation. In the eyes of international opinion, most Arab states, and many Palestinians, the Israeli military was starting to withdraw and was allowing for greater Palestinian autonomy. Israel's international reputation was restored, as the country was seen to have made peace.

Israeli and Palestinian Responses to the Oslo Accords
The Oslo Accords were a major achievement for the Israeli government: the Palestinian "tiger" had become the "horse" that would bear the burden of managing its people's internal affairs. Furthermore, Oslo II agreed that, pending a final, permanent status agreement, Israel would retain control of most of the land, its resources, and overall security matters. The Palestinians in the West Bank were now largely corralled into small, self-governing districts.

Initially, the accords elicited widespread support in Israel. It seemed that "normalization" had been restored after the turbulent years of the intifada, and Israel was now more widely accepted on the international stage. Many Israelis felt that the Palestinian problem had been solved.

The accords also won much popular support among Palestinians. The PLO was recognised by Israel and the rest of the international community as "the sole representative of the Palestinian people," and Israeli forces began to withdraw from Palestinian cities. Sara Roy, an American academic, wrote:

> Joy and hope returned . . . with the signing of the Oslo agreement. I was in Gaza City when the Israeli army redeployed from the urban areas of the Strip in May 1994. The freedom to walk their streets without fear or harassment left Palestinians ecstatic. That night, Gaza City's main commercial street throbbed with thousands of people, many in their finest clothes. . . . There were dancers and singers. The stores were open, food was free, and children had all the chocolate they wanted. The city was a swirl of light and color.[6]

The PA became internationally recognised as a political entity, and for the first time in the twentieth century, the Palestinians had their own government in a part of historic Palestine. Arafat returned to Palestine for the first time since 1948 and was met by cheering crowds when he arrived in Gaza in July 1994. The PA adopted the flag and the national anthem of the PLO.

A Palestinian police force was established and many PLO fighters, who had been deported to Tunis in 1982, returned and were incorporated into this force. In 1994, Israeli forces were withdrawn from Jericho and, toward the end of 1995, from five further West Bank cities. In January 1996, Palestinians voted for their own parliament, the **Palestine Legislative Council (PLC)**, while Arafat was elected as president of the PA.

Many Palestinians were encouraged by the ebullient Arafat, who assured his people that the Oslo Accords committed Israel to the creation of an independent Palestinian state. Data from a poll conducted by the Center for Palestine Research and Studies (CPRS) in Nablus in August and September 1995 showed 71 percent support for the peace process.[7]

The Decline of the Peace Process

Despite this early optimism among both Israelis and Palestinians, the Oslo peace process had almost completely collapsed by 2000.

There were many reasons for this. First and foremost, Oslo represented an agreement between two very unequal partners – a militarily powerful Israel and a much weaker Palestinian body. This imbalance was shown most clearly in the unequal timing of concessions made by the two sides: while the Israelis were granted what they most needed (security and an end to the intifada) in the first Oslo Accord, the Palestinians would have to wait for what they most wanted (the removal of settlements, a state of their own with East Jerusalem as its capital, and the resolution of the refugee issue) until further negotiations were completed. Israel now had less incentive to make further concessions, while, in recognising Israel, the Palestinians gave up 78 percent of historic Palestine and one of their few remaining levers in negotiation – the use of violence.

Furthermore, in Oslo II, the delineation of Area C left Israel in direct control of the aquifers and much of the most fertile land in the West Bank. As it was also agreed that Israel would build a network of "Israeli only" bypass roads that linked Israeli settlements to each other and to Israel, over 250 miles of roads were built on confiscated Palestinian land in succeeding months. These roads enabled Israel to divide and fragment Palestinian-controlled lands so that little contiguity existed between them. This left many Palestinians feeling that they were living in small, isolated islands in a sea of Israeli-controlled land and that the occupation was becoming more entrenched than ever. As would become clear in the years ahead, this diminished the likelihood of a viable Palestinian state emerging.

While the Oslo Accords initially won widespread support among both Israelis and Palestinians, a few public intellectuals, such as the Palestinian American Edward Said and the Israeli Meron Benvenisti, characterised the accords respectively as a "capitulation"[8] and a "surrender"[9] by the Palestinian leadership. "The occupation continues," wrote Benvenisti, "albeit by remote control and with the consent of the Palestinian people, represented by the PLO."[10] Moreover, Palestinian maintenance of public order, the efficacy of which Israel would be the judge, would be the precondition for the staged withdrawals of the IDF from further Palestinian population centers. This would preserve Israeli control of security on the whole of the West Bank.

On both sides, opponents of the Oslo agreements were quick to denounce what they saw as a betrayal of their principles. On the Israeli side, opponents included members of the Likud Party and the settlers' council, who argued that none of Judea and Samaria should be given up and that settlers' lives were put at risk by Israeli troop withdrawals.

On the Palestinian side, the "rejectionists" included Hamas and other smaller groups who thought that the Palestinians gained little from the accords, as there was no Israeli recognition of the Palestinians' right to an independent Palestinian state, let alone the promise of such a state. Hamas refused to recognise Israel or support a two-state solution. It declared the Oslo agreements to be a "historic act of treason."

The five-year period that was built in to the timetable for peacemaking provided plenty of opportunity for opponents to sabotage what was seen, by critics on both sides, as a flawed process. In February 1994, Baruch Goldstein, an American-born Jewish settler, entered the Ibrahim Mosque in Hebron and killed twenty-nine Muslim worshippers. Palestinians blamed the Israeli government for not disarming the settlers and for allowing this to happen. They pointed out that Israeli settlers had the army and police to protect them, as well as being heavily armed themselves, and that most Palestinians felt very vulnerable.

Support for Hamas increased dramatically after the Hebron massacre. Two months later, Hamas exploded a car bomb at a bus stop in Israel, killing eight people. Over the next few years, Hamas embarked on a campaign of suicide bombings, both in the occupied territories and in Israel itself.

The Rabin government began to harden its stance, especially in the face of Hamas militancy and a public that was becoming increasingly skeptical about the efficacy of the Oslo Accords in enhancing Israeli security. Some Israelis suspected that Arafat was using the establishment of the PA on Palestinian soil as a launchpad for the destruction of the State of Israel. So intense was opposition to the Oslo peace process in some Israeli quarters that, at one demonstration, an effigy of Rabin wearing a Nazi uniform was held aloft.

The Israeli government blamed Arafat and the PA for not controlling the militants. Israeli troops moved back into areas in Gaza and the West Bank that they had recently left. Curfews were imposed in the towns, cities, and refugee camps. The Israelis closed the border crossings between Israel and the occupied territories to prevent suicide bombers from slipping through. Roadblocks and checkpoints prevented Palestinians from traveling easily between regions controlled by the PA. These "liberated" areas became, as many Palestinians described, a series of big prisons.

Despite these setbacks, talks between the Israeli government and the PA still went ahead, often abroad. Agreements were made to withdraw Israeli troops from more Palestinian towns and cities on the West Bank, and in return, Arafat agreed to arrest Hamas militants. But, time and time again, it was extremists on both sides who dominated the headlines.

In November 1995, 150,000 Israelis gathered in Tel Aviv for a peace rally. The main speaker was Prime Minister Yitzhak Rabin, who had signed the peace deal in 1993. After the rally, a young Israeli, Yigal Amir, stepped up and shot Rabin, who died on the way to the hospital. The assassin was a member of an Israeli group that opposed any peace with the Palestinians. This group believed that the West Bank was part of the Land of Israel, the land that God had promised to the Jews. In their view, Rabin had been prepared to give away parts of the sacred Land of Israel and was thus a traitor to the Jewish people. At his trial, Amir said, "When I shot Rabin, I felt I was shooting a terrorist." He was sentenced to life imprisonment.

Most Israelis supported the peace process. Many believed that it was worth exchanging land for security and many accepted that one day there would have to be a Palestinian state based in the West Bank and Gaza. The assassination of Rabin was a heavy blow to the peace process.

However, it was a series of suicide bombings carried out by Hamas in Jerusalem and Tel Aviv in February and March 1996 that did the most to transform the political climate in Israel. In May 1996, a Likud-led government, hostile to the Oslo process, was elected.

In February 1997, the new Israeli government, headed by **Benjamin Netanyahu**, gave the go-ahead for the building of 6,500 new homes on Arab land in East Jerusalem. This would complete a chain of Jewish settlements around the eastern side of Jerusalem, effectively cutting off the Arab inhabitants of East Jerusalem from the rest of the West Bank. This further dented Palestinian hopes of making East Jerusalem the capital of an independent Palestine. As the bulldozers

An Israeli bulldozer demolishes an Arab house on the West Bank to make way for a larger Jewish settlement, February 1997.

began to clear the ground for building, the new Israeli prime minister announced, "The battle for Jerusalem has begun."

The West Bank and Gaza After Oslo

Nothing did more to erode Palestinian confidence in the Oslo process than the continued growth of Israeli settlements. Settlement building, or at least the expansion of existing settlements, continued, although the Israelis and Palestinians had agreed during the Oslo discussions "that neither side shall initiate or take any step that will change the status of the West Bank and Gaza pending the outcome of the permanent status negotiations."

Even while Israel appeared to the world as if it were negotiating peace with the Palestinians, it "was simultaneously expanding not only its settlements but also the extensive infrastructure of roads, electricity, water, and phone lines needed to sustain them."[11] Such was the dramatic increase in settlement activity that the number of settlers on the West Bank increased by 70 percent, from 115,000 to 200,000, in the years from 1993 to 2000. The Israeli government continued to claim that "security" and "military needs" justified settlement expansion.

Much settlement building was carried out according to local initiatives and circumstances. However, there was much more consistent government support, particularly from 1996 to 1999, when the Likud leader, Benjamin Netanyahu, was prime minister. Many more outposts were established by "hilltop youth," who proved to be more radical, lawless, and violent than their Gush Emunim predecessors in the 1970s. Settler attacks on the Palestinians continued and, in the villages, many Palestinian families were too frightened to harvest their olives and sank further into poverty.

An Israeli soldier points his gun at a Palestinian man and his family at the north entrance to the West Bank city of Hebron.

Together with continued settlement building, and the land confiscation and house demolition that it entailed, Israel maintained the separate supplies of water and electricity for Jewish settlements as it had before Oslo. It also continued to maintain separate legal systems for Jewish and Palestinian inhabitants of the West Bank and Gaza – Israeli civilian law for the former and military law for the latter. Israeli occupation laws and military orders remained in force. The use of curfew, deportation, arrest, and torture remained fundamental methods of maintaining Israeli control of the West Bank and Gaza, while thousands of Palestinians, including children, continued to be brought before Israeli military courts every year.

Above all, Israel's military domination of the West Bank undoubtedly intensified after Oslo, nowhere more so than on the periphery of the Palestinian cities of Area A. This is largely explained by the fact that the Israeli government left it to the IDF to conduct Israeli withdrawals from land that was being evacuated and the chief of staff, **Ehud Barak**, saw every piece of land handed over to the PA as "a potential springboard for future attacks on Israel."[12] He thus planned and built new army bases, bypass roads, and roadblocks to surround that land. Settlement perimeters were expanded, and tighter control exercised over neighbouring Palestinian communities. Most Palestinians had expected the Oslo process to end the military occupation, but instead Oslo became an instrument for enhancing it.

The Economy of the Occupied Territories after Oslo

The architects of the Oslo Accords had believed that much of their success would rest on an improvement in the economic conditions and the standard of living of Palestinians in Gaza and in the West Bank. Linked to the Oslo Accords was the Paris Protocol of 1994, which promised an "open economy" with free movement of goods and labour and economic regeneration for the Palestinians in the occupied territories.

In practice, however, it entrenched the methods by which Israel controlled the economy of the territories, only this time by agreement. The Palestinians were still denied the right to establish their own currency, and Israeli goods continued to have unrestricted access to the West Bank, while the trade in Palestinian goods to Israel was restricted by tariffs.

After Oslo, and especially after Palestinian suicide bombings, Israel reduced its dependence on Palestinian labour and employed more migrants from the Far East. The subsequent loss of income was a major cause of the sharp fall in the Palestinian standard of living. In 1994, 30 percent of the Palestinian workforce in the West Bank was employed in Israel, whereas in 1996, the figure was down to 18 percent.[13] Nevertheless, access to a supply of cheap labour remained a "tap" that could be turned on or off by the Israelis, a further illustration of their continued and increased domination of the Palestinian economy.[14]

The Paris Protocol also agreed that Israel would collect import or customs duties on goods destined for the occupied territories and then pay them monthly to the PA. From 1995 to 2000, 60 percent of total PA revenue came from this source. Yet it could be cut off at will by the Israelis. In 1997, for instance, the Israeli government voted to halt the transfer of funds after a series of bombings. This meant that Palestinian teachers, doctors, nurses, and civil servants could not be paid. In this way, pressure or punishment could be administered by the Israelis.

In the Oslo Accords, Israel was granted the right to implement "closures" to the crossing points into Israel and Israeli-controlled Area C, prohibiting Palestinians from entering. From 1994 to 1999, Israel imposed 484 days of closures and installed as many as 230 temporary or "floating" checkpoints.[15] Such restrictions had been used during the First Intifada, but they were now institutionalised. The Palestinian economy became a hostage to closures and checkpoints.

The constraints placed on the Palestinian economy by the Paris Protocol undoubtedly contributed to the increase in unemployment among Palestinians in the territories – it rose from 15 percent in 1993 to 30 percent in 1995.[16] They also increased the financial problems encountered by the PA in maintaining public services such as schools, hospitals, and social welfare.

Eager to support the peace process and enable the inexperienced PA to build new administrative structures and pay for the salaries of public servants, the international community stepped in. Between 1994 and 2000, the European Union (EU), national governments, and NGOs provided $3.2 billion to the West Bank and Gaza, equivalent to the combined GDP of the two areas.[17]

In effect, international donors bailed out the PA, making it dependent on them. In this way, part of the cost of Israel's occupation was subcontracted to the international community. Israel was relieved of the financial burden of supporting Palestinian education, health, and other public services after Oslo, and foreign governments and agencies became complicit in the new regime and effectively lent international endorsement to an occupation that, in international law, was illegal.

An Inefficient and Corrupt Palestinian Authority
As the Palestinians in the occupied territories became increasingly frustrated and impatient with the lack of progress made in the Oslo peace process, they also became more critical of the behavior of the PA. Local leaders, the "insiders," many of whom had been prominent in popular committees during the First Intifada, were sidelined by returning members of the PLO.

The so-called Tunisians, the members of the PLO who had been in exile with Arafat in Tunis, were appointed by him to the top posts in the administration. Most of them had little knowledge or firsthand experience of the disruptive and destructive nature of the Israeli occupation. Furthermore, the health and welfare services provided by the PA were often seen as inferior in quality to those that had been organised by the local leadership during the First Intifada.

Moreover, some of Arafat's closest colleagues built large villas and were suspected of siphoning money donated for state building by foreign governments. A small capitalist class benefited from its close relationship with the PA, securing permits to import and export, and monopoly rights on goods such as fuel, building materials, flour, and tobacco. In this way, Oslo enabled the Israelis to secure a cohort of willing collaborators: Palestinians with a vested interest in the continuing partnership between Israel and the PA. As one Israeli official said, "We control everything. There are a number of natives who serve as middlemen. What could suit our purposes better?"[18]

One of Yitzhak Rabin's main reasons for devolving responsibility for internal Palestinian security onto the PA had been his view that "the Palestinians will be better at it than we were ... They will rule by their own methods, freeing, and this is most important, the Israeli army soldiers from having to do what they [the Palestinians] will do."[19]

Arafat did, undoubtedly, employ his "own methods," using his security forces to arrest and imprison hundreds, perhaps thousands, of Palestinian opponents of the Oslo Accords, some of them from lists drawn up by the Israelis. However, Arafat was keen to avoid overt conflict between his own security forces and groups like Hamas, as this would be highly divisive. Besides, he did not wish to be seen as Israel's policeman.

The Israeli public and its leaders accused the PA of not doing enough to curb the extremists. The usefulness of the PA as a "partner" in managing the Palestinian population was increasingly being doubted by members of the Israeli government. By the late 1990s, Israel's faith in the peace process was waning. Even Yossi Beilin, one of the Israeli architects of the Oslo Accords and a champion of Israeli-Palestinian negotiations, reported that he had told **Mahmoud Abbas**, the chief PLO negotiator:

> Any future Palestinian state must be demilitarised, that the Israeli army will stay on the Jordan River, that there will be no return to the 1967 borders, that the Palestinian refugees from 1948 will not be permitted into sovereign Israel, that Jerusalem will not be redivided, and that the Jewish settlements will not be uprooted.[20]

It seemed that Israel was shutting out further negotiation and foreclosing discussion on the "final status" issues of a permanent settlement and that, for them, the Oslo Accords represented a final, not an interim, settlement. An Israeli vision of limited autonomy for the Palestinians appeared to be prevailing over a Palestinian vision of national self-determination.

Nevertheless, under intense US pressure, Israeli-Palestinian talks did continue. In June 1997, it was agreed that Israeli troops would be withdrawn from the West Bank city of Hebron. Further talks, held in September 1998 in the US, led to agreement on further Israeli troop redeployment. However, at the same time, Ariel Sharon, now foreign minister, called on West Bank settlers to "Move, run and grab as many hilltops as you can to enlarge settlements because everything we take now will stay ours."[21]

Camp David, 2000

By 2000, the Oslo process had reached an impasse. In the Israeli elections of 1999, only two of the twelve competing parties spoke of the need for peace negotiations, such was the widespread lack of urgency or interest, certainly for the immediate future. However, the newly elected Labour

Prime Minister Ehud Barak, President Bill Clinton, and Yasser Arafat at Camp David, 2000. Despite the smiles, it proved impossible to agree on a peace deal.

government, under Ehud Barak, had pledged to revive negotiations with the Palestinians.

In July 2000, Barak and Yasser Arafat were summoned to Camp David in the United States by President Bill Clinton, who was determined to have one last attempt to break the deadlock. Barak realised that his coalition government was already falling apart, and he abandoned the "piecemeal approach" approach of the Oslo process and staked everything "on a last throw of the dice."[22] He offered Arafat "a non-negotiable, take-it-or-leave-it" final settlement.

What Barak called his "generous offer" covered the substantive issues of land, settlements, refugee rights, and Jerusalem, even agreeing to the partition of the latter. Barak offered the Palestinians over 90 percent of the West Bank, as well as all of Gaza, which would allow the Israelis to continue to control nearly 10 percent of the West Bank territory that contained the biggest Israeli settlements. (The idea of a land swap, whereby the Israelis would hand over some of their own land in return for annexing some West Bank land, was also discussed at Camp David, although there was no agreement on whether it would be an equivalent amount.)

As the Palestinians saw it, they had already given away 78 percent of historic Palestine by recognising the State of Israel within the pre-1967 borders, and yet here was Israel proposing to annex almost 10 percent of the West Bank. Moreover, the Palestinians were asked to put aside what had been negotiated at Oslo and accept Israeli assurances of good faith.

The latter, however, was asking a lot. Israel had consistently failed to meet its commitments to withdraw troops or halt settlement growth. A further obstacle to peace was the issue of refugees: Israel was prepared to allow a small number to return for family reunification but would not concede to the Palestinian demand that Israel recognise its responsibility for the dispossession and expulsions in the *Nakba* of 1948–49.

The talks finally foundered on the issue of Jerusalem, with the Palestinians demanding exclusive sovereignty over the Arab suburbs and, above all, of the Muslim holy sites on the Haram al-Sharif compound (Temple Mount to Jews). Arafat said, "I prefer to die than to agree to Israeli sovereignty on Haram. I'm not going to enter the history of Arabs and Muslims as a traitor."[23]

The Palestinians have been justifiably criticised for coming unprepared to the talks and for not offering a counterproposal of their own for negotiation. However, what Barak offered was, in effect, "peace by ultimatum" – there would be no time for further discussion.[24] In the aftermath of Camp David, he persuaded most Israelis that the Palestinians had, by rejecting his offer, shown that they were no longer fit to be partners in peace, and, by implication, the whole basis of the Oslo Accords was undermined.

Two months later, Ariel Sharon embarked on a tour of Haram al-Sharif/Temple Mount and provided the catalyst for the outbreak of a second, more violent intifada. "Trust between the two sides broke down completely. The Oslo Accords were in tatters," wrote Avi Shlaim.[25]

Personal Testimony
Amos Oz

Amos Oz was an Israeli writer and a founder of Peace Now, an Israeli organisation that campaigned for an end to the occupation and for a two-state solution. Here, he recollects his views after Israel's victory in 1967 and after Oslo in 1993:

In June 1967, when I returned from war in the Sinai Desert to Jerusalem, what I saw was not David's capital. I saw the Arab shoeshine boy looking at me fearfully. And I remembered my childhood in British Mandate Jerusalem and the intimidating, surly British soldiers. I understood that although Jerusalem is my city, it is a foreign city. I knew I should not rule over it, that Israel must not rule over it. Old Jerusalem is our past, but it is not our present, and it endangers our future ...

I realized that what I saw in Jerusalem, others did not see. Both the Right and mainstream Labour thought of 1967 as the completion of 1948. What we were not strong enough to do then, we were strong enough to do now. What we didn't conquer then, we conquered now. I thought that state of mind was dangerous. I realized that the West Bank and Gaza Strip are the Palestinians' poor man's lamb. I knew we must not take it. Not one inch, not one settlement. We must keep the territories only as a surety until peace is reached ...

By the early 1990s it was all very different. Reality had struck and changed both Israelis and Arabs. The 1973 [Yom Kippur] war made the Arabs realize that they could not take us by force. The 1987–92 uprising made the Israelis realize there is a Palestinian people, and they will not go away. They were here and they were here to stay. After a hundred years of mutual blindness we suddenly saw one another. The illusion that the other would disappear was gone. That's why the views held by only a handful of Israelis after the Six-Day War were eventually adopted by the majority. Peace had moved from the fringes to the very center.

When Peres sent me a draft of the Oslo Accords, I saw the problem. I understood that in reality, what we had here was a tricky tripartite agreement between the government of Israel, the PLO, and the settlers. But still I thought it was a good beginning. I believed Oslo would bring down the cognitive wall separating Israelis and Palestinians. And once the wall came down, there would be progress.

We would advance step by step toward a true historic conciliation ...

I made one big mistake. I underestimated the importance of fear. The Right's strongest argument is fear. They don't say it out loud because they are ashamed to, but their most compelling argument is that we are afraid. It's a legitimate argument. I, too, am afraid of the Arabs. So if I were to start the peace movement all over again, that's the one change I would make. I would address our fear of the Arabs. I would have a genuine dialogue about the Israeli fear of extinction.[26]

Sari Nusseibeh

Sari Nusseibeh is a Palestinian academic, activist, and writer. Here, he explains how terror and settlement building went hand in hand in the years after Oslo.

The spread of settlements both precipitated and followed Palestinian terrorism ... In January 1995, a month after the Nobel ceremony [where Arafat, Rabin, and Peres were jointly awarded the famous Nobel Peace Prize], Rabin promised Arafat to halt new settlements and to confiscate Arab land only for roads. Three days later came another terrorist attack, and Israel suspended negotiations. Three days after that – less than a week after Rabin made his promise to Arafat – the Israeli cabinet approved building an additional 2,200 housing units in the West Bank.

And so it went. That summer, Hamas bombed two more Israeli buses, while the Rabin-Peres government adopted the "Greater Jerusalem" master plan, which included more construction on an outer ring of Israeli settlements extending deep into the West Bank.

No one in Israel was listening to Palestinian protests because Hamas terror was creating a frenzied atmosphere in Israel that people likened to civil war. Tens of thousands of [Israeli] anti-Oslo protesters crowded the squares in Jerusalem. Neither Rabin's legacy as the "bone-breaker" nor the dizzying sums he spent on settlement "security" and expansion lessened their loathing for him and his peace plan. Palestinian terror and Israeli hostility to Oslo went hand in hand.[27]

Anita Shapira

Anita Shapira is an Israeli historian. Here she explains how talks at Camp David in 2000 broke down over the issue of Jerusalem.

The most difficult issue of all was Jerusalem. Relinquishing sovereignty over all of Jerusalem was contrary to everything the Israelis had said since 1967. Repartition of Jerusalem was an idea that no Israeli leader had previously uttered. But now Barak rose to the challenge. He was prepared to offer the PA the outer Arab neighborhoods in East Jerusalem, the Muslim and Christian Quarters in the Old City, and even to give Arafat custodianship of Haram al-Sharif. The Israelis would retain the Jewish neighborhoods built after 1967, the Jewish and Armenian Quarters in the Old City, the Western Wall, and sovereignty over the subterranean Temple Mount. By any yardstick, Barak's proposal was revolutionary. But Arafat would not even consider it. Unlike his American and Israeli interlocutors, Arafat was in no rush. While Barak displayed tremendous courage, in the end he was unable to convince Arafat that there was no chance of further concessions. And perhaps Arafat feared that making any concession on Jerusalem would enrage Muslims throughout the world and even lead to his being assassinated.[28]

CHAPTER 9

From the Second Intifada to War in Gaza

2000–08

This chapter examines the impact of the Second Intifada and events in Gaza on the Palestinian-Israeli conflict.

- **Why did the Second Intifada break out in 2000?**
- **Why did Israeli forces evacuate Gaza in 2005?**
- **What was the impact of Hamas's rise to power?**

The Second Intifada, 2000–05

On September 28, 2000, Ariel Sharon, now leader of the Likud Opposition Party, made a tour of what Jews call Temple Mount and Muslims call Haram al-Sharif. Both Jews and Muslims regard this area of Jerusalem as sacred. For Jews, it is the site where they believe the first and second temples once stood. For Muslims, it is the location of the Dome of the Rock and the al-Aqsa Mosque (see image on p. 39), which are, by agreement with the Israeli government, cared for by an Islamic religious trust. Sharon obviously expected trouble, as he was accompanied by nearly a thousand police.

The visit was seen by Palestinians as a highly provocative move. Many saw it as a threat to impose Israeli control over the Muslim holy sites. Sharon may have wanted to assert the Jewish right to pray on the Mount or, as the new Likud leader, he may have wanted to upstage Netanyahu, his chief rival in the party. It is more than likely that he also wished to embarrass Ehud Barak for having shown willingness to negotiate over the sovereignty of the holy sites at Camp David. He undoubtedly wished to demonstrate his opposition to any negotiations over the status of Jerusalem and Israel's "undeniable sovereignty over the entire united Jerusalem."[1]

Whatever his intentions, demonstrations followed, and the next day, when Palestinians threw stones over the Wailing Wall at Jewish worshippers below, Israeli troops shot four Palestinians dead and wounded over two hundred. The unrest spread across the West Bank and Gaza. This marked the start of the Second Intifada, often known as the "al-Aqsa Intifada." It was to last five years and four thousand were to be killed – three thousand Palestinians and one thousand Israelis.

Initially, it was mainly an unarmed uprising characterised by nonviolent protest, but 1.3 million bullets were fired in the first month by Israeli troops. Whether or not the security forces overreacted or, as some Israelis and many Palestinians believe, wished to fan the flames to justify a harsh military response, 127 Palestinians were killed in that period.

Sharon's visit undoubtedly triggered the start of the Second Intifada, but the underlying cause was the frustration and anger of the Palestinians in the occupied territories. Seven years on from the Oslo Accords, little progress had been made. The number of settlers had soared and, for many Palestinians, living conditions had worsened and the daily humiliations of living under occupation had increased.

The Palestinians felt more hemmed in than ever. In Gaza, a strip of land between the sea and the Israeli border, just twenty-five miles long and nowhere more than seven miles wide, there were nearly 1.5 million Palestinians, half of them in refugee camps dependent on UN handouts. Among them were eight thousand Jewish settlers with fifty thousand troops protecting them. They controlled a third of the land and most of the water supplies.

On the West Bank and around Jerusalem, there were nearly four hundred thousand Jewish settlers. There were over two million Palestinians on the West Bank, but the Israelis controlled over 70 percent of the land and had complete control of the water and electricity supplies. They also controlled the main roads, which most Palestinians were forbidden to use, and they restricted the movements of all Palestinians with the use of checkpoints and nighttime curfews. Sari Nusseibeh, a Jerusalem resident, described the situation in his city:

> While settlers were flooding into the West Bank, a series of fortified roadblocks tightened the noose round Jerusalem by choking off access to Palestinians from the West Bank. Only those with hard-to-get special permits were allowed to pass the checkpoints. Needless to say, settlers zoomed past without question. Palestinians who had worked in Jerusalem found themselves jobless, and students, patients, and worshippers couldn't get to schools, hospitals, or religious sites.[2]

The Israelis seemed to be consolidating their hold on the land. A permanent peace and an independent Palestinian state seemed more distant than ever. Furthermore, many Palestinians had lost confidence in the PA's ability to secure any benefits from the peace process, and promises of liberation and a better life seemed hollow.

On the third day of the intifada, a twelve-year-old Palestinian boy, Mohammed al-Dura, was shot dead by a sniper while sheltering behind his father. No doubt there were similar occurrences elsewhere, but this one was caught on camera by a French photojournalist and shown on Al Jazeera television across the Arab world and many times on Palestinian television. Two weeks later, two Israeli soldiers took a wrong turning in Ramallah, were arrested by Palestinian police, and then lynched by a mob that invaded the police station where the men were being questioned. Again, this was caught on camera, this time by an Italian film crew. The horror of events like these led to calls for vengeance on both sides and intensified the frenzy of public opinion.

The Israeli military carried out incursions into Palestinian cities and tightened restrictions on movement. They set up roadblocks, often by placing huge lumps of concrete at the entrances to Palestinian towns and villages, to curb travel in and around the West Bank.

In 2002, the military reintroduced permits, which were required for travel within the West Bank. A study by the World Health Organization found that between September 2000 and December 2004, sixty-one Palestinian women gave birth while being kept waiting at checkpoints and thirty-six of the newborn children died of complications that could not be treated on the roadside.

In November 2000, the Israelis carried out the first of their "targeted assassinations." Using helicopter gunships, they fired rockets to kill those they suspected of inciting violence. The targets were often members of Hamas, **Islamic Jihad**, or militant factions of Fatah. While many attacks showed pinpoint accuracy, others led to the deaths of the militants' family members, and women and children nearby.

In March 2001, Sharon became prime minister in a landslide election victory for his Likud Party. Nicknamed "the Bulldozer" by Israelis, he was, for Palestinians, the man who had carried out the massacre at Qibya in 1953 (see p. 104). He was also held responsible for the massacre of Palestinian refugees in Sabra and Shatila in 1982 and, as housing minister in the early 1990s, he had overseen the most intense program of settlement building to date.

For the historian Avi Shlaim, Sharon was the arch proponent of the philosophy of the "iron wall" promulgated by Vladimir Jabotinsky in the 1920s (see p. 32). Believing that the Palestinians would never willingly accept a Zionist state, Jabotinsky had insisted that only an iron wall of military strength would force the Palestinians to acquiesce.[3]

Sharon now wished to use Israel's overwhelming strength to impose his own unilateral solution on the Israeli-Palestinian conflict. He viewed Arafat as the instigator of the intifada, not as a partner in peacemaking, and had no wish to negotiate – let alone compromise with the Palestinians over settlements – the status of Jerusalem and the refugees' right of return.

Suicide Bombings and "Targeted Assassinations"

In March 2001, militant Palestinian groups, chiefly Hamas, started a campaign of suicide bombings inside Israel – on buses, in restaurants, and in other public places. An increasing number of Palestinians believed that this was a weapon, perhaps the only weapon, that could counter Israel's overwhelming military superiority. One of the most shocking attacks was on a nightclub in Tel Aviv that killed twenty-one people, mostly teenagers, in June 2001.

The aftermath of a Hamas bus bombing in West Jerusalem, 2004

If the symbol of the First Intifada was the teenager throwing stones, the symbol of the second was the suicide bomber. Far more weapons were used by Palestinians in the Second Intifada, but far fewer Palestinians were actively involved.

The Israelis responded to the nightclub killings by intensifying the policy of assassinating those they accused of masterminding the bombings, especially members of the Hamas leadership, but it did nothing to halt the attacks. The cycle of suicide bombings and assassinations escalated.

The Israeli sociologist Baruch Kimmerling wrote of how the reactions of both Israeli Jews and Palestinians to suicide bombing showed the "inability of each to understand its opponent":

> The Israeli Jews see the phenomenon as the ultimate proof of the cruel, zealous and primitive Palestinian nature and conclude that it is impossible to engage in reasonable negotiations with people who send their children to kill both themselves and innocent

people ... This lack of understanding has blinded most of the Israeli population to the poverty, the life-long harassment and humiliation, the hopelessness, and the perpetual violence and killing that blight so many Palestinian lives and lead so many young Palestinians to such desperate acts ... The same lack of empathy has also blinded Palestinians to Jewish grief and anger when suicide bombers massacre innocent civilians, emotions that are intensified when many Palestinians publicly express their happiness after every successful operation.[4]

The Impact of 9/11

In September 2001, attacks carried out in the United States reverberated around the world, and nowhere more so than in the Middle East. Nineteen men, mostly from Saudi Arabia, hijacked four US passenger planes and crashed two of them into the World Trade Center in New York City. Over three thousand people were killed; these are known as the events of 9/11, the date on which they occurred.

Weeks later, President George W. Bush launched a "War on Terror." He was determined to wipe out al-Qaida, the organisation thought to be behind 9/11, and its leader, Osama bin Laden.

In its response to suicide bombings, the Israeli govern-ment now presented Palestinian resistance, specifically that of Hamas, as a form of international terrorism, like al-Qaida. Fur-thermore, Sharon blamed Arafat, declaring to the Americans, "You have bin Laden, we have Arafat." He accused Arafat of bearing the responsibility for continuing Palestinian violence.

Historians are divided as to whether Arafat was unable or unwilling to rein in the militants. Certainly, Hamas and Islamic Jihad rejected his leadership, as did some Fatah members. Meanwhile, in pursuit of his own war on "terror," Sharon told his army chief of staff "to strike at the Palestinians everywhere . . . simultaneously. The Palestinians should wake up every morning to find out that twelve of them are dead."[5] In April 2002, President Bush referred to Sharon as "a man of peace."

Operation Defensive Shield, 2002

In March 2002, in the single most deadly attack, a Palestinian suicide bomber killed twenty-nine people in a hotel in Israel. Two days later, Sharon launched Operation Defensive Shield, a long-prepared invasion and reoccupation of the main towns in the occupied territories to "root out the terrorist infrastructure."

Using tanks, fighter jets, helicopters, and thirty thousand troops, the IDF destroyed much of the political and social infrastructure that had been built by the PA, often with foreign aid, in the years since Oslo–government buildings, radio and television stations, water and electrical facilities. The IDF blew up houses suspected of harbouring militants; arrested, tortured, and imprisoned thousands of Palestinians; imposed day-long curfews; and closed schools and universities.

The PA security forces largely fled and there was little armed resistance, but when the Israelis decided to invade the refugee camp in Jenin, which they saw as a breeding ground for "terrorists," they met fierce resistance from Hamas and other fighters. To reduce the threat of ambush and booby traps in the narrow streets and alleyways of the camp, the Israelis used armored bulldozers to cut swaths through the closely packed houses.

Susan Nathan, a British Jew who had moved to Israel, visited Jenin with Palestinian friends and later wrote:

> After visiting Jenin, I was unprepared for the horrifying details of what had taken place, and of the terrible destruction wrought on the inhabitants' lives as well as on the centre of Jenin camp. Watching the survivors, broken-hearted amid the rubble of their homes, hopeless and with an understanding that their voice would never be properly heard, I felt their rage. It dismayed me to realize that I too was seeing the Israeli army, full of those "good Jewish boys," as a terrorist army, and that for the first time I was beginning to understand the emotions that can drive a suicide bomber to action, I could see how unfair it sounds to a Palestinian to hear a suicide bomber being labelled a terrorist when we refuse to do the same if an Israeli soldier bulldozes a house with a family inside.[6]

Fifty-two Palestinians and twenty-three Israeli soldiers were killed in Jenin. Four thousand Palestinians were made homeless as whole blocks of the camp were destroyed. In Ramallah, Arafat's compound, the Muqata, was left in ruins, with power and phone lines cut. The Palestinian president lived under virtual house arrest until his death, two years later. In May 2002, the Israeli military forces withdrew from Palestinian cities, although they stayed nearby and continued to make arrests, carry out house searches and demolitions, and impose curfews.

The Separation Barrier

Sharon continued to insist that the Palestinians had no wish to negotiate – there was no partner for peace. In fact, he spurned a Saudi peace proposal that was supported by all the Arab states, and several plans that were formulated by individual Israelis and Palestinians meeting privately.

One of the latter plans garnered over three hundred thousand signatures, from both Israelis and Palestinians. It was made by Sari Nusseibeh, the Palestinian president of Al-Quds University in Jerusalem, and Ami Ayalon, former head of Shin Bet, the Israeli internal security agency.

Sharon, however, was determined to pursue an Israeli-imposed solution. In June 2002, work started on the building of a barrier around the West Bank. Called the "security fence" by the Israelis and the "separation wall" by the Palestinians, it was, in some places, a twenty-five-foot-high concrete wall; in other places, it was just a fence. It was reinforced by troops, barbed wire, watchtowers, and CCTV cameras.

Israelis said the barrier was temporary to keep out the bombers, but its opponents argued that if it was purely defensive it would have followed the **Green Line** that marked the pre-1967 boundary between Israel and the West Bank. Instead, it cut deep into the West Bank to incorporate the largest Israeli settlement blocs on the Israeli side.

In addition to the many West Bank Jewish settlements on the Israeli side of the wall were some Palestinian villages. This land, about 10 percent of the West Bank, was effectively being annexed. The Israelis were creating "facts on the ground," making it far less likely that any future Palestinian state would include all of the West Bank.

The Israeli security barrier separating East Jerusalem
from the Palestinian village of Abu Dis

When the barrier was finished, twenty-seven thousand
Palestinians would find themselves living between the
barrier and the Green Line. They were cut off from family
and friends on the other side. Farmers were cut off from their
land, patients from hospitals, children from their schools,
only able to cross through one of the checkpoints in the
barrier after obtaining special permits – and, even then, only
at specified times. The Israelis could pass through, without
stopping, on bypass roads (their cars had differently colored
number plates).

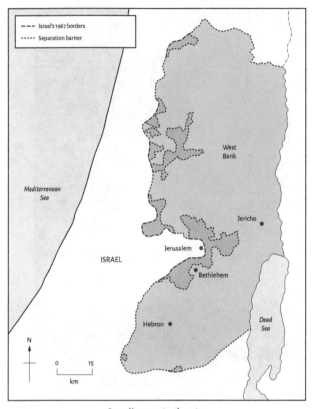

Israel's security barrier

Some Palestinians dubbed it the "**apartheid** wall," indicative of the comparisons increasingly being made between Israel and white-dominated South Africa. The International Court of Justice criticised the wall whenever it cut into the West Bank and ordered building to stop. It didn't.

Far fewer Israelis were killed in Palestinian suicide bombs after the construction of the barrier (130 in 2003 and fewer than 25 in 2005), convincing most Israelis that it saved the lives of fellow Israelis and was necessary for their security. However, the decline in bombings can also be attributed to the permanent presence of Israeli troops inside and around Palestinian cities and increasing security cooperation between the IDF and the PA, particularly after the Second Intifada ended in 2005.

The Israeli Evacuation of Gaza, 2005

In April 2003, President Bush came up with the "Roadmap for Peace," backed by the EU, UN, and Russia in the so-called **Quartet**. The map envisioned a Palestinian state alongside Israel.

Sharon accepted, keen to maintain the support of the one world leader who, in his view, really mattered. However, he also countered with a plan of his own. In December 2003, he surprised both Israeli and international public opinion by coming up with a plan for "disengagement," for pulling back Israeli settlers and troops from Gaza.

Gaza was a huge burden for Israel: overcrowded, impoverished, and a Hamas stronghold. It tied down fifty thousand troops to protect its eight thousand Jewish settlers. The settlers in Gaza and many advocates of a Greater Israel were opposed to Sharon's plan, while some supporters of the peace process thought that this might be followed by a gradual withdrawal from the West Bank.

For Sharon, his move would steal the initiative, sideline Arafat, and win international support. Above all, being so dramatic and unexpected, it might preempt US pressure to implement the Roadmap, thus preventing any need for compromise over the future of East Jerusalem, the settlements, or the Palestinian refugees' right to return, all of which the Roadmap entailed.

It is not known whether Sharon intended to withdraw from parts of the West Bank but, to his supporters, he stressed that the evacuation of Gaza would be accompanied by a strengthening of Israel's control "over those same areas in the Land of Israel [i.e., in the West Bank] which will constitute an inseparable part of the State of Israel in any future agreement."[7] In other words, it was a trade-off – Gaza in exchange for the West Bank.

Before implementing his plan, Sharon sought a reward from Bush for his offer of withdrawal from Gaza. In April 2004, Sharon secured US guarantees on two issues. First, that in any future peace agreement the six biggest blocs of Israeli settlements in the West Bank would be incorporated *within* the borders of Israel. Bush assured him:

> In light of new realities on the ground, including already existing major Israeli population centers [i.e., the big Israeli settlement blocs], it is unrealistic to expect . . . a full and complete [Israeli] return to the [1967] border.[8]

Bush also guaranteed that Palestinian refugees of 1948 would not be allowed back to their original homes but would be absorbed in a future Palestinian state "rather than in Israel."

The Israeli government got what it wanted on both borders and refugees, while two of the Palestinians' most cherished ideals – Israeli withdrawal to the 1967 borders and the **"right of return"** – were denied. These two assurances represented a reversal of what had been US policy since 1967 and destroyed any remaining credibility that the US might have had as an honest broker in resolving the Israeli-Palestinian conflict. To Arafat, Bush's guarantees were simply "a new Balfour Declaration."[9]

In late summer 2005, the settlers were evacuated from Gaza and Israeli troops were withdrawn. The settlement buildings were demolished. The disengagement from Gaza won international applause, derailed the Roadmap, and eased the pressure on Israel to reach a compromise on the West Bank settlements. As Sharon's adviser, Dov Weisglass, said in an interview:

> The significance of our disengagement plan is the freezing of the peace process ... It supplies the formaldehyde necessary so there is no political process with the Palestinians ... When you freeze the process, you prevent the establishment of a Palestinian state, and you prevent a discussion on the refugees, the borders, and Jerusalem. All with [American] presidential blessing and the ratification of both houses of Congress.[10]

The Israelis continued to exercise remote control over Gaza. They controlled the movement of people in and out of the territory and the supplies of water, fuel, and electricity. They would only allow fishermen to travel six nautical miles from the coast of Gaza, not twenty miles as had been agreed at Oslo. Above all, Israelis controlled the airspace, which meant that they could monitor Palestinian actions on the ground, continue to carry out aerial bombardment and assassinations, and interfere with radio and television broadcasts.

Under international law, "effective control by a hostile army" – which the Israelis continued to exercise in Gaza – constitutes occupation.[11] In this view, Gaza continued to be land occupied by Israel.

The Death of Arafat

Sharon often spoke of the need to "remove" Arafat, although we do not know whether he meant politically or physically. What we do know is that Arafat's health deteriorated throughout 2004. He finally agreed to be evacuated to a hospital in Paris in October and died two weeks later, at the age of seventy-five.

Arafat was viewed negatively by most Israelis and, especially after the failure of the Camp David talks in 2000, as an obstacle to peace by the United States and some Western governments as well. He lived frugally and worked tirelessly to win recognition for the PLO as the sole, legitimate representative of the Palestinian people, and from 1988, he was committed to a two-state solution. He made mistakes, including his failure to rein in the extremists in Jordan in 1970 and his support for Saddam Hussein in 1990. Yet, he had largely created the Palestinian national movement and led it for nearly half a century.

In 1993, he ended the PLO's years of impotent exile in Tunisia and established a Palestinian government on Palestinian soil after negotiating the Oslo Accords. Moreover, as Avi Shlaim writes:

> Arafat understood the asymmetry of power, the difficulty for his people of negotiating their way out of an occupation by diplomatic means alone when the occupier was determined to hold on to their land.[12]

Under Arafat's leadership, the PLO was, in its early years, a clandestine, underground liberation movement, but it proved less able to make the transition to state building and transparent governance that was required of the PA. The PA was characterised by organisational and financial mismanagement, with competing, overlapping agencies and individual ministers making their own private deals. As leader, and one who exercised a very personal power, Arafat must bear the prime responsibility for much of this. At his death, the future of the Palestinian cause seemed more uncertain than ever.

Arafat was succeeded as president by Mahmoud Abbas, who won 62 percent of the vote in elections held in January 2005. Abbas was committed to diplomacy and continuing talks with Israel.

The Rise of Hamas

Before the evacuation of Gaza, the Israelis had attempted to destroy much of the Hamas leadership so that the organisation could not claim victory after the Israeli withdrawal. In 2004, Israeli forces killed the movement's spiritual leader, Sheikh Yassin, in a missile attack, and followed this by assassinating his successor and several others.

Hamas supporters at the funeral procession of Sheikh Yassin

However, the militants proved resilient, and in September, after the Israeli withdrawal, they fired twenty-nine rockets into Israel, claiming that the Israeli withdrawal from Gaza was a victory for "armed resistance." In January 2006, Hamas achieved a dramatic and unexpected victory over Fatah when elections were held for the Palestinian Legislative Council (PLC), the Palestinian parliament. How can this dramatic electoral success be explained?

Hamas had come to prominence with its campaign of suicide bombing in the 1990s and, even more so, during the Second Intifada. Not surprisingly, it was designated a terrorist organisation by Israel, the United States, and, later, by governments in the EU. Hamas opposed the Oslo Accords and, in particular, the PA's coordination of security arrangements within the occupied territories with the Israelis. This Israeli-PA policy led to the arrest and detention, in PA-run prisons, of many from Hamas and the much smaller Islamic Jihad. Nevertheless, most Palestinians continued to support the PA and its policy of negotiating, even at the height of the Second Intifada, with the Israelis.

The main problem for the PA was that cooperation with Israel brought little tangible benefit. Most obviously, it failed to end the occupation. Settlement building in the West Bank continued, closures and checkpoints multiplied, and Palestinians' movements were ever more severely restricted. The economy of both the West Bank and Gaza suffered, with dramatic consequences. In 1999, 20 percent of Palestinians in the occupied territories were deemed to be in poverty (defined as living on less than $2.10 a day), but by 2003 it was 60 percent.

Support for Hamas grew, both in Gaza and the West Bank, as Palestinian disillusionment with the Fatah-dominated PA increased. Abdel Aziz Rantisi, a pediatrician and one of the founders of Hamas, contrasted Hamas's policy of resistance with the PA's strategy of negotiation, which, he said, represented a "life of humiliation [under] a despicable occupation."[13]

Hamas justified its attacks on Israel as a form of self-defence against what it saw as an inherently violent and illegal military occupation. Hamas espoused Islamic ideals, and its long-term aim, according to its charter, was to establish an Islamic state in all of Palestine. However, it put far more emphasis on its national goals, particularly on its short-term objective of achieving a Palestinian state in the occupied territories, including East Jerusalem.

The organisation took credit for having "liberated" Gaza from Israeli military control, yet neither its support of armed struggle nor its Islamic ideology figured prominently in campaigning for elections to the PLC in 2006. Instead, Hamas candidates highlighted the need for "change and reform," pointing out that Fatah-led PA rule had not brought law and order or economic recovery since Israel's disengagement from Gaza. They exploited the resentment and frustration felt with seemingly endless and, as they saw it, failed peace talks, and called for a leadership and a national strategy that was free from Israeli and US control and could resist the occupation.

With unemployment and poverty rates soaring, they called for programs to provide food, education, health, and welfare facilities. Here, Hamas's reputation for clean, efficient administration, as shown in their charitable provision of schools, orphanages, clinics, and hospitals for Christians as well as Muslims, won much support. Above all, Hamas campaigned against the corruption at the heart of the PA administration.

Hamas won 74 of the 132 seats across the occupied territories. Mahmoud Abbas remained as president of the PA, but he invited Ismail Hanieh, a Hamas leader from Gaza, to become prime minister and to form a cabinet. Talks were held with a view to forming a government of national unity, containing both Hamas and Fatah members. What would be the reaction of Israel, the United States, and the international community?

The West's Response to Hamas's Election Victory
The US government had long been proclaiming the need for democratic governments in the Middle East. Furthermore, international observers declared that the elections had been free and fair. Nevertheless, the United States and Israel were quick to condemn the establishment of any Palestinian government in which Hamas played a part.

The EU initially supported dialogue with Hamas, respecting it for having participated in democratic elections and believing that, within a unity government, Hamas would be pragmatic enough to engage in peace negotiations. The EU, however, soon fell in behind the US and, under further pressure, all the members of the Quartet – the United States, the EU, Russia, and the UN – agreed to lay down three conditions that Hamas had to meet if the PA was to continue to receive financial assistance: first, renunciation of violence; second, formal recognition of Israel; and third, acceptance of all previous Israeli-Palestinian agreements.

The first was difficult for Hamas to agree to since it believed it was engaged in a just war and had a legitimate right to resist what international law deemed to be an illegal occupation. On the second, Hamas, in its statements and policy, had effectively recognised Israel in acknowledging the desirability of a two-state solution. However, it proved unwilling to formally recognise Israel until Israel had withdrawn from the occupied territories. On the third, Hamas refused to endorse the Oslo Accords, which had, in its opinion, largely served to entrench the Israeli occupation and render the PA subservient to Israel.

Most Palestinians wanted a unity government, while an opinion poll in September 2006 found that as many as 67 percent of Israelis supported negotiations with such a Palestinian government.[14] However, the Israeli government, supported by the United States and the EU, had clearly decided that the Palestinians had voted for the wrong party. As Gaza resident Adeeb Zarouk told journalist Donald Macintyre, "The whole world wanted us to have democracy and said how fair had been our election. The problem is that they didn't like our results."[15]

The PA president, Mahmoud Abbas, and his Fatah colleagues were eager to follow the path of diplomacy, continuing negotiations on "final status" issues along lines laid down in the Oslo Accords and the Roadmap. They also wished to continue to receive financial aid from the United States and EU to promote economic growth. Nevertheless, Fatah members joined a Hamas-led government in March.

The Israeli government responded by withholding the payment of customs revenues that, under Oslo, Israel collected at its ports on goods imported by the Palestinians and then handed on to the PA. The United States also cut aid that went directly to the PA. In April, the EU followed suit. Thousands of PA employees – teachers, healthcare workers, civil servants – could not be paid.

Living conditions, particularly in Gaza, deteriorated as Israel's blockade was tightened and Gazans were no longer able to cross into Israel to work as day labourers. Gaza also experienced widespread lawlessness because of clashes between the security forces of Hamas and Fatah vying for control.

Suffering was intensified in June 2006 when Israel launched an attack, by land and air, in response to Hamas rocket fire and the capture of an Israeli soldier. Gaza's only power station was destroyed, reducing electricity supplies for seven hundred thousand people. The power station was eventually repaired by international donors, but this was to be the start of the daily power cuts, often lasting for eight hours or more, which continue to this day. For much of its electricity, Gaza remained dependent on Israeli supplies that could be, and regularly were, cut.

Tension remained high between Hamas and Fatah. The Saudis brokered a peace between the rival parties in February 2007 and Hamas's leader Khaled Mashal spoke of "preparedness to accept a Palestinian state on the 67 borders."[16] However, Israel and the United States deliberately undermined the Palestinian unity government. They financed and trained the Abbas security forces in readiness for a coup to overthrow Hamas. Hamas got wind of this, and in a week of savage fighting in June 2007, their militias overcame Fatah's forces in Gaza. Hamas forces seized all Fatah bases in Gaza and established sole control over the area.

Abbas dissolved the unity government and formed a new, Fatah-led government to rule the West Bank separately. The US and EU resumed their aid and Israel resumed its payment of customs revenues to the PA government in the West Bank. Hamas was isolated, and Gaza was declared a "hostile entity" by Israel. Despite frequent attempts at reconciliation, the Palestinian national movement remains split to this day.

Israeli-Palestinian Peace Talks, 2008

Even at times of heightened tension, peace negotiations between Israel and the PA continued intermittently. In 2008, direct talks were held in the United States between PA President Mahmoud Abbas and Israeli Prime Minister Ehud Olmert. (Olmert had succeeded Ariel Sharon when the latter fell into a coma in 2006.)

At no time, before or since, have the two sides made more concessions in the search for a lasting peace. They agreed on the need to partition Jerusalem, while Olmert held out the prospect of a Palestinian state on 93.5 percent of the West Bank. In return for keeping the 6.5 percent of the area that contained the main Israeli settlement blocs, he offered the Palestinians almost as much land in Israel in exchange. Olmert agreed to accept five thousand Palestinian refugees as part of a family reunification program, but not as an acknowledgement of the right to return.

George W. Bush with Ehud Olmert (left) and Mahmoud Abbas (right)

Abbas wanted Israel to take in 150,000 refugees over the course of ten years. Although a larger number, it was only a fraction of the five million UN-registered refugees in camps in the region, which many Palestinians would undoubtedly see as giving up the demand for the right to return. Abbas, himself a refugee from 1948, recognised that it was "illogical to ask Israel to take five million, or indeed one million. That would mean the end of Israel."[17]

The major sticking point was Israel's insistence on keeping the settlement of Ariel, which extended into the heart of the West Bank, and all the settlements around Jerusalem. Nevertheless, the talks represented a serious desire for lasting peace on both sides.

Whether differences could have been ironed out is unknowable. Certainly, both leaders would face huge opposition for having given away too much. As it happened, both leaders were in weak positions domestically: Abbas had just lost control of Gaza and Olmert was facing trial for corruption. (He would later be found guilty and imprisoned.) The talks fizzled out and, with the outbreak of war over Gaza in December 2008, were never resumed.

Israel's War in Gaza, 2008

While West Bank Palestinians benefited from international aid and experienced economic growth, Gazans endured increasing hardship while intermittent Palestinian rocket fire into Israel continued to be met by Israeli missiles. Then, in December 2008, Israel launched Operation Cast Lead.

Its forces had long planned for a campaign of supposedly pinpoint bombing of Hamas bases, military stores, training camps, and the houses of senior Hamas officials. Its declared aim was self-defence: to stop Palestinian rocket fire and weapons smuggling. However, on the first day, Israeli forces killed forty police cadets during their graduation parade[18] and over the course of the three-week campaign, an estimated 1,400 Gazans were killed, of whom 900 were civilians, including over 300 children.[19] Thirteen Israelis were killed, four of them mistakenly by their own troops. According to the UN, over four thousand houses and six hundred factories were destroyed.

A UN investigation, led by a South African judge, Richard Goldstone, found both sides guilty of committing war crimes: Hamas and other militant groups had deliberately harmed civilians, while Israel was judged to have carried out deliberate attacks "not justified by military necessity" on many nonmilitary targets. The UN report concluded that Israel's action was "a deliberately disproportionate attack designed to punish, humiliate and terrorise a civilian population."[20]

Nevertheless, despite the use of overwhelming power, Israel failed in halting rocket attacks on southern Israel. If Israel had aimed to drive Hamas from power, it also failed. Gazans may have suffered immeasurably, but Israeli hopes that they would rise and topple the Hamas government were not realised. The Israeli blockade was tightened. The importing of materials – cement, steel pipes, and industrial equipment – needed for the reconstruction of Gaza was banned on the grounds that the materials could be used to build bunkers or weapons.

A resolution of the Israeli-Palestinian conflict seemed further off than ever. However, the election of **Barack Obama** as US president in 2008 raised international hopes for a resumption of peace negotiations.

Personal Testimony

This Israeli sergeant spent much of his military service seeking approval for Palestinians to secure health care in Israel, which was unobtainable in the West Bank. His fellow soldiers teased him for being a "social worker." He opposed the occupation and the way Palestinians were controlled and humiliated, but in 2002, he said that Israel had done what was necessary. Four years later, he spoke of and reflected on his army service.

Defensive Shield had to be done like that. Right then. We could not wait any longer. The bombings were intolerable and if one had waited any longer, we would have looked weak. Mistakes were made, yes, but we had to strike. We cannot ever afford to appear weak …

It is very hard to see these people [the Palestinians] suffer. You just had to help them. But sometimes you got fed up and couldn't listen to their stories any more. Of course, you do see them as people. But they were different because at the end of the day, you finish your duty and go back to your base, or go home and leave it behind, and I always tried to have a clear conscience …

A soldier was killed, and the next day I went to his funeral. It's basically, "The enemy shot my friend, and now I'm helping them [Palestinians] through my checkpoint." You have a hostile population and armed soldiers on the other side. We haven't yet got to the point where we realize the occupation is bad for us. [21]

Ari Shavit

Israeli Ari Shavit wrote of the shock wrought in Israel by the campaign of Palestinian suicide bombings from 2001, and then of Israelis' restored confidence when it was largely ended by 2004:

> The wave of terrorism that rattled their cities for three years reminded Israelis where they lived and what they faced. But under the leadership of the old-time warrior Ariel Sharon, Israel rose to the challenge. After their initial surprise, the IDF and Shin Bet [security agency] waged a sophisticated and effective counteroffensive. Israeli society proved to be far more resilient than expected. By 2004, Israel managed to stop suicide terrorism. The result was euphoria, and a regained sense of security and self-assurance that led to an economic boom. The 2005 unilateral pull-out from Gaza – the disengagement – was also initially perceived as a success and contributed to the general sense of safety. The generals agreed that our strategic position had never been better, and as Israel grew more and more prosperous, the nation was once again pleased with itself and intent on celebrating its dolce vita.[22]

Raja Shehadeh

Writing in 2008, Raja Shehadeh, a Palestinian, expressed the fear among West Bank Palestinians that they were "unwanted strangers" in their own land:

Such was the power of ideology that in the eyes of most Israelis, "Israel" had come to mean "the Greater Land of Israel," including most of the settlements. In fact, maps used in Israeli school books had done away with the pre-1967 borders between Israel and the Occupied Territories. To defend their "country" also meant to defend the settlements in the Occupied Territories. In its decisions, the Israeli High Court confirmed this. The settlers, it ruled, had a basic right to be protected by the state. The fact that they were on illegally acquired land made no difference …

The large number of checkpoints and obstacles placed by the Israeli army on West Bank roads complicated our lives immeasurably. Even after the bombing in Israel had stopped, they increased in number from 376 in August 2005 to 528 by October 2006. We now moved in our own country surreptitiously, like unwanted strangers, constantly harassed, never feeling safe. We had become temporary residents of Greater Israel, living on Israel's sufferance, subject to the most abusive treatment at the hands of its young male and female soldiers controlling the checkpoints, who decided on a whim whether to keep us waiting for hours or to allow us passage. But worse than all this was that nagging feeling that our days in Palestine were numbered and one day we were going to be victims of another mass expulsion.[23]

CHAPTER 10

Palestinians and Israelis in the Age of Netanyahu

2009–PRESENT

This chapter examines developments in Israel and Palestine during the time of Prime Minister Benjamin Netanyahu.

- Why did hopes for a lasting peace recede during Obama's presidency?
- What was the impact of the war in Gaza in 2014?
- What was the significance of Israel's Nation State law of 2018?
- Why was President Donald Trump's "Deal of the Century" applauded by many Israelis but rejected by Palestinians?

Netanyahu and Obama

There was worldwide sympathy for Palestinian suffering during the Israeli invasion of Gaza in 2008 but in Israel there was overwhelming support for the country's military actions, which were seen as taken in self-defence.[1] (The influence of the Israeli Left, those who called for an end to the occupation, continued to decline, as it had done since the suicide bombings of the Second Intifada.)

Elections held in February 2009 led to the formation of the most right-wing government in Israeli history. Prime Minister Netanyahu had overwhelming support from the increasingly powerful settler lobby, represented by the Yesha Council, and he renounced his predecessors' peace proposals. He was committed to the concept of Greater Israel, to the continued colonization of land in the West Bank and the expansion of settlements in and around East Jerusalem. His uncompromising approach won him numerous reelections.

When President Obama took office in January 2009, many people entertained hopes of a breakthrough to peace. Obama believed that settlement building was the single greatest obstacle to any agreement between Israel and the PA. He let Netanyahu know, in no uncertain terms, that he regarded settlement building as "illegitimate." However, Netanyahu knew that he could defy the US president and not pay any political price because of the strength of the US's "Israel lobby," largely made up of Jews and the far more numerous **Evangelical Christians** (many of the latter believe that Christ's second coming will only occur when all Jews have returned to the "Land of Israel" – i.e., the biblical land, including Judea and Samaria).

The influence of this lobby, in turn, did much to explain why the US Congress remained unwaveringly pro-Israeli and kept voting for financial and military aid (as of 2023, over $3 billion annually) to Israel. So consistently strong was US support for Israel that, between 1978 and 2010, the United States exercised its right of veto on the UN Security Council in order to block resolutions that were critical of Israel on forty-two occasions.[2] (Any one of the five permanent members of the Security Council – the United States, Russia, China, Britain, and France – has the power of veto.)

Meanwhile, Mahmoud Abbas, the head of the PLO and the PA, faced deadlock in his relations with both Hamas and the Israeli government. This may explain why he continued to look to the United Nations for support, especially as he hoped that the United States under Obama might be less obstructive than under Bush. In 2011, Britain, France, and Germany drafted a UN Security Council resolution condemning Israeli settlements. However, the United States used its veto for the first time during the Obama presidency, thus preventing its adoption. (The US government believed that passing the resolution would make the Israelis less likely to resume peace talks.)

Abbas did, nevertheless, secure a diplomatic breakthrough a year later when the UN General Assembly (which represents all members and votes by simple majority) recognised Palestine and granted it the status of a "non-member state with observer status" (similar to the Vatican). By mid-2020, 130 out of 193 member states had recognised the state of Palestine.

This diplomatic victory made no difference to the reality on the ground. In fact, Netanyahu's response was a plan to build more settlements on a stretch of land that would effectively bisect the West Bank. Even when Secretary of State John Kerry persuaded the two sides to reopen peace talks in 2013, Netanyahu still would not agree to freeze settlement building. (The Palestinians feared that Israel was engaging in peace talks simply to appease international opinion and play for time while extending Israel's reach into the West Bank.) Netanyahu continued to insist that settlements played a vital role in Israel's security. However, as recently as 2012, a report by retired Israeli military and security experts had concluded that "the settlement project not only does not contribute to the overall security of the State of Israel" but that it was the military, not the settlements, that increased security.[3]

In 2014, the Israeli NGO Peace Now reported that, during nine months of negotiations, Israeli settlement building had increased fourfold with the planning or construction of nearly fourteen thousand homes in the West Bank and East Jerusalem. The organisation reported that this settlement activity "created facts on the ground that proved more than anything else that the Netanyahu government did not mean to go for a two-state solution."[4] In particular, the plans to expand Jewish settlements in occupied East Jerusalem would end hopes of ever dividing the city between Israelis and Palestinians and of having a viable Palestinian capital in Jerusalem. Hopes of any kind of peaceful resolution of the conflict receded even further with the outbreak of war in Gaza in the summer of 2014.

War in Gaza, 2014

In June 2014, Fatah and Hamas were reconciled and reached agreement on the formation of a Fatah-dominated government. Although not a single member of Hamas was to be included in this government, Netanyahu accused Abbas of allying with "terrorists" and again halted the transfer of customs revenues to the PA.

Then, later the same month, three Israeli teenagers from a West Bank settlement were kidnapped and killed. Hamas was immediately blamed by the Israeli leadership, although the organisation had not ordered the killing, and over 350 Hamas supporters in the West Bank were arrested and imprisoned by Israeli forces. The crisis escalated when a Palestinian teenager was kidnapped in East Jerusalem and burned to death. Rockets were fired from Gaza into Israel and Israel launched airstrikes.

So began a war that was to last seven weeks, consisting of over six thousand Israeli air strikes and a major ground invasion of Gaza. Whole neighbourhoods were destroyed, and water and electricity supplies were cut. Palestinian rockets reached further than previously – with one landing near Tel Aviv's airport – but most were intercepted by Israel's highly effective Iron Dome anti-missile system.

According to the Israeli human rights group **B'Tselem**, over two thousand Palestinians were killed, most of them noncombatants, while sixty-seven Israeli soldiers and five civilians were killed. The campaign, especially the deaths and maiming of children, attracted massive international coverage but disappeared from the headlines once the fighting was over. The United States and its European allies asserted that "Israel has a right to defend itself."

Hamas claimed a "victory of the resistance" (the death toll among Israeli troops was far higher than expected) but failed to end Israel's blockade of Gaza. If anything, it became tighter: restrictions on the imports of foods were designed to allow Gazans just enough food to survive and no more. (A leaked US diplomatic cable stated that the aim of the blockade was to "keep the Gazan economy on the brink of collapse without quite pushing it over the edge."⁵) Gazans continued to suffer intense hardship, but neither the war nor the blockade made them turn against their leaders.

Netanyahu claimed a military success as Israel destroyed many of the tunnels that extended into Israel. But this did not stop continued smuggling of weapons through tunnels under the Gaza-Egypt border. It certainly failed to eliminate Hamas as a military and political force. However, the Israeli government claimed that its campaign had weakened Hamas militarily and would later argue that the steep decline in rocket attacks from Gaza in the following two years was proof of its deterrent effect. For some Israelis, this showed how necessary it was to "mow the grass" in Gaza every few years.[6]

Most Israelis supported the campaign in Gaza (over 90 percent in one poll).[7] Moreover, in 2015, they reelected Netanyahu at the head of a coalition government that included members of the far-right Jewish Home Party, whose leader called for the annexation of the whole of Area C in the West Bank (see p. 159).

In 2017, the Israeli parliament passed a law to "regularise" the status of Jewish "outposts" that had been built on private Palestinian land in the West Bank. Israeli opponents condemned what they saw as a "land grab" and even the president of Israel said it made Israel "look like an apartheid state."[8] Critics of the regime also singled out the Nation-State Law of 2018, in this case for its mistreatment of Israel's Arab citizens.

Arab Israelis and the Nation-State Law, 2018

The Arabs of Israel, those who remained in the State of Israel after 1948, made up approximately 20 percent of the population by 2018. They have long been the odd man out in the Palestinian-Israeli conflict, receiving less attention than Palestinian Arabs in the occupied territories and refugee camps, and lived under Israeli military law until 1966 (see p. 92).

Since 1967, when all of historical Palestine came under Israeli control, Israeli Arabs have increasingly come to see themselves as Palestinian citizens of Israel. After 1967, they could share common experiences of Israel's policy, involving loss of land and other forms of discrimination, with fellow Palestinians in the occupied territories. Nevertheless, while the Palestinians of the occupied territories have focused on ending the occupation since 1967 and establishing a

Palestinian state, the Palestinian citizens of Israel have prioritised their struggle for equality within the State of Israel.

Palestinian Israelis possess the democratic right to vote, and in 2015, they won thirteen of the 120 seats in the Knesset, the Israeli parliament. However, they have experienced discrimination in many other areas. This has been particularly significant in land and housing. While hundreds of new towns and villages have been constructed for Jewish citizens of Israel since 1948, planning permission has not been granted for a single new Arab town or village. The threat of loss of land and house demolition has hung over Palestinian Israelis.

In 1967, when Israel took control of the West Bank and Gaza, free movement between Israel and the newly occupied lands had become possible. Palestinian Israelis could visit family and friends in the West Bank and Gaza and vice versa. There were marriages between Palestinians from different sides of the pre-1967 border.

Palestinian Israelis increasingly identified with the wider Palestinian community. Many Israelis feared what they saw as the "Palestinization" of Arab Israelis, seeing it as a sign of disloyalty. However, opinion polls have consistently shown that while most Palestinian Israelis support the creation of a separate Palestinian state, they also show that the majority wish to remain Israeli – only with equal rights – and not to move to any future Palestinian state in the West Bank and Gaza.

Palestinian Israelis have become more assertive in recent decades. In March 1976, the impending confiscation of land in the Galilee region, in northern Israel, as part of the Israeli state's campaign for the "Judaization of the Galilee," led to a general strike and the outbreak of demonstrations. Six protesters were killed on what became known as Land Day and which has been commemorated by the Palestinian citizens of Israel since 1988.

In 2000, anger erupted in response to news of the shooting of Arabs in East Jerusalem at the start of the Second Intifada. There were widespread protests, demonstrations, and stone throwing: thirteen Arab protesters were killed by police and hundreds arrested.

Then, starting in 2011, Palestinian Israelis began to commemorate *Nakba* Day – in memory of the disaster that struck their ancestors in 1948 – on the day after the Jewish Israelis commemorate their Day of Independence. Many walked to the sites of their ancestral homes, often only a few miles away. However, in 2017, the Israeli government banned the public observance of *Nakba* Day. It seemed to many that only the historical narrative of the winners was to be observed.

Israel's Nation-State Law, 2018

In July 2018, Israel passed the Nation-State Law, which declared:

> The Land of Israel is the historical homeland of the Jewish people, in which the State of Israel was established … The right to exercise national self-determination in the State of Israel is unique to the Jewish people.

As well as stating categorically that only Jews in Israel possessed the right to "national self-determination," it downgraded the Arab language of Israel's Palestinian citizens from an official language to one of "special status." Not surprisingly, Palestinian Israelis opposed the law because it entrenched

Palestinians wave Palestinian flags on Nakba Day, the day after Israel's Independence Day, 2010.

their inferior and marginalised status in law. They were joined by many liberal Jews, who claimed that it was undemocratic, and in confining Israel's Arab citizens to the status of second-class citizens, it was making Israel into an "apartheid state." As Galia Golan, a Jewish member of the Knesset, said of the law, "It amounts to sending a message to your minority, that was here to begin with, that they have no place here."[9]

In addition, the law ran counter to Israel's 1948 Declaration of Independence, which stated that Israel would "ensure complete equality of social and political rights to all its inhabitants irrespective of religion, race or sex." It seemed that the law was declaring that it was more important for Israel to be Jewish than to be democratic.

Palestinian Israelis continue to strive for equal rights within Israel. Above all, they overwhelmingly believe, as do most Palestinians, that a lasting peace between Israelis and Palestinians, whether the latter live in Israel, the occupied territories, or in the wider diaspora, must be based on an acknowledgement

217

by Israel of its role in creating the *Nakba*, the dispossession, dispersal, and expulsions of 1948. As Ayman Odeh, a Palestinian Israeli member of the Knesset, said in 2016, "I try to feel the historical pain of the Jewish people – the Holocaust, the pogroms. I'm asking Jews to feel my historical pain."[10]

President Trump's "Deal of the Century," 2020

In passing the Nation-State Law, the Israeli government was undoubtedly emboldened by the arrival of **Donald Trump** at the White House.

Even before he had taken office in January 2017, the newly elected president made clear his pro-Israeli stance – and his disregard for international law – when he said he would recognise the whole of Jerusalem as Israel's capital. Then he chose David Friedman, a financial supporter of West Bank settlements, as US ambassador to Israel. Friedman had previously told a meeting of Israeli settlers that Israel should annex the West Bank.[11]

President Trump and Prime Minister Netanyahu in Jerusalem, May 2017

Trump knew that his stance on Israel would win wide approval among Evangelical Christians, who made up a significant portion of his electoral base. Within months of taking office in January 2017, Trump announced that his government would produce a comprehensive Israeli Palestinian peace settlement. He claimed it would be "the deal of the century." His son-in-law, Jared Kushner, whose family donated money to Israeli settlements, was put in charge of negotiations.

Trump's plan was not fully revealed until January 2020, but much of it was foreshadowed by steps that his government took in the preceding two years:

- In May 2018, the US Embassy in Israel was transferred from Tel Aviv to Jerusalem and Trump declared that the issue of Jerusalem was "off the [negotiating] table." This broke both long-held US policy and international law, which stated that the Israeli annexation of East Jerusalem in 1967 had been illegal and the status of Jerusalem should be determined by a final resolution of the Palestinian Question.

- In September 2018, the United States announced that it would end all its funding of the PA and UNRWA, which looks after Palestinian refugees.

- In February 2019, the US government ordered the closure of the Palestinian Mission (in practice, the embassy) in Washington, DC, on the grounds that the Palestinians had not done enough to further peace.

- In November 2019, the United States announced that it no longer considered Israeli settlements "necessarily illegal."

Encouraged by this climate, Netanyahu announced in 2019:

> I am guided by several principles when it comes to the West Bank. The first: this is our homeland. The second: we will continue to build and develop it. Third: not one resident or community will be uprooted in a political agreement. Fourth: the Israeli military and security forces will continue to rule the entire territory up to the Jordan Valley.[12]

It appeared that he was to be granted his wishes when, in January 2020, details of the plan were finally announced by Trump in Washington. Key points were:

- The Jordan Valley to be annexed on the grounds that it was necessary for Israel's security.
- Israel to incorporate the vast majority of settlements into contiguous Israeli territory, which would result in the annexation of over 30 percent of the West Bank.
- The Palestinians to be offered a state of their own with its capital in the town of Abu Dis on the outskirts of Jerusalem.

Annexation of the Jordan Valley, the Palestinian "breadbasket," and of Israeli settlements contravened international law and numerous UN Resolutions, the most recent of which was adopted by the Security Council in December 2016 and stated that settlements in the West Bank were in "flagrant violation" of international law. (Passed in the final days of Obama's presidency, the United States had abstained in this vote. Trump's plan argued that annexation of the settlements reflected the facts on the ground, which the international community had failed to reverse. (Arguably, the US bore the prime responsibility for the failure.) In effect, he was presuming to legitimise the reality on the ground, thus giving Israel a green light to annex huge swaths of Palestinian territory.

The plan claimed to be a two-state solution because it offered the Palestinians a state of their own, made up of Gaza and a series of enclaves, scattered and disconnected, in the West Bank, with some parts of Israel's Negev Desert to be included as compensation. Yet the Israeli state would retain sole control over the security of the West Bank and its network of roads, tunnels, and military bases.

Palestinians would have even less access to the valuable agricultural land and water resources of the Jordan Valley needed to feed their population centers. The Palestinian capital would be in the town of Abu Dis, several miles from the Old City of Jerusalem and on the eastern side of the wall. Furthermore, the Palestinian state would be demilitarised, have no borders with neighbouring Arab states, and have no control over its own skies, borders, or water resources. It would have to recognise Israel as a "Jewish state" and agree not to seek legal redress for Israeli war crimes in the UN or International Criminal Court. Refugees would receive "some compensation."

As an inducement to accept the plan, the Palestinians were offered a huge economic aid package, to be funded by US allies in the Gulf (notably Saudi Arabia, Bahrain, and the UAE). The Palestinian president, Mahmoud Abbas, responded by declaring that Jerusalem and Palestinian rights were not for sale.

All the Palestinian factions rejected the plan: it effectively destroyed any prospect of a viable, sovereign Palestinian state. The Israeli government knew that the Palestinians would reject the plan and this would enable them to portray the Palestinians as rejectionist and to continue with their policy of de facto annexation. Not surprisingly, the plan was applauded by the Israeli government and the settler movement in particular, as it fulfilled nearly all their demands.

Within Israel, there was considerable support for the plan. It represented a significant move toward the normalization of the Israeli occupation and the proposed annexation was entirely consistent with the Zionist objective, as enunciated by David Ben-Gurion, of creating and maintaining a predominantly Jewish state in as much of Palestine as possible.

However, it was not without its critics in Israel. Many Israelis were not won over by Netanyahu's argument that the plan would enhance Israel's security: they feared that it would further weaken President Abbas and the PA and increase support for Hamas, while the annexation of the Jordan Valley might destabilise relations with the neighbouring state of Jordan. There was widespread resentment of the influence of the more extreme, militant settlers. The most forthright critic was probably the journalist Gideon Levy. Writing in *Haaretz*, the Israeli newspaper that is most consistently critical of Israeli government policy, he declared:

This is their [the Palestinians'] third *Nakba*. After losing most of their land, property and dignity in the first and their liberty in the second [in 1967], now comes the third to crush whatever is left of their hope. Diplomatic struggle and armed struggle, non-violent protest and economic boycott. Nothing has helped.

Israel gets everything and without conditions, while the Palestinians, a fairly restrained people given the terrible abuse it endures, still have to prove themselves in order to receive the little crumbs of justice that the American president throws to them.[13]

The Israeli government announced plans to annex parts of the West Bank beginning in July 2020, but this plan was subsequently postponed. However, all of the land between the Mediterranean and the Jordan River was increasingly becoming one state, made up of 6.6 million Jews, 1.8 million Israeli Palestinians with citizenship but restricted rights, and 4.8 million Palestinians (in East Jerusalem, the West Bank, and Gaza) with no citizenship and few rights. This one-state reality, in which Palestinians would soon outnumber Israeli Jews, not only denied Palestinians their internationally recognised right to self-determination, but also threatened Israel's future as a majority-Jewish and democratic state.

Daily Life in the Occupied Territories

West Bank

The landscape of the West Bank has been transformed by the Israeli Army and, above all, by settlement building. In Area C, which now makes up over 60 percent of the area, Israel controls much of the best agricultural land, water resources, and mineral wealth. In November 2023, there were over 700,000 settlers in the West Bank and East Jerusalem. The major settlements are now sizable towns with shopping centers, parks, and swimming pools.

Most settlers live close to the Green Line (the pre-1967 border) and commute to work in Israeli cities by day. Many are attracted by cheap housing, loans, and tax exemptions. However, an increasing number of "religious nationalist" Israeli Jews have established settlements, often deep inside the West Bank. These settlers, often young and militant, are committed to the building of *Eretz* Israel, a Greater Israel that incorporates all of what used to be biblical Judea and Samaria. They justify settlement in religious terms, seeing it as "the bedrock of Jewish national identity."[14]

A rising number of settler attacks on Palestinian people and property have been documented by the UN, as well as by Israeli and Palestinian human rights groups. The Israeli government has been reluctant to intervene in the face of growing settler militancy. Meanwhile, the IDF continues to demolish Palestinian houses and other property in Area C on the pretext that they have been built without the required permits and to imprison thousands of Palestinians every year (over four hundred thousand since the occupation began in 1967, including more than twenty thousand children). Checkpoints and roadblocks in the West Bank can turn half-hour journeys into far longer ones and make it impossible to plan how long a journey will take.

Most Israelis learn little from their media of the daily life of the Palestinians, and opinion polls suggest that they are less concerned than ever about the fate of the Palestinians. They feel safer behind the Separation Wall and see few, if any, Palestinians in their daily lives. The West Bank Palestinian writer, Raja Shehadeh, asks:

> Is it any wonder that the Israelis don't see us when Israel has orchestrated a life of separation between the two nations, with different roads for each, a wall separating the two sides and warning signs on roads leading to Palestinian cities and villages lest Israelis wander in by mistake? And when Israel has changed the law to make it possible for Israelis to settle in most parts of the territory and violate the rights of Palestinians to property and personal protection with impunity, while expecting the Palestinian security forces to cooperate with them in restraining Palestinians from attacking Israeli forces or Jewish settlers?[15]

The separation of Israeli Jews and Palestinians in the West Bank is reinforced by Israeli laws. For instance, Jews in the West Bank are governed by civilian law and tried in civilian courts, whereas Arabs are subject to Israeli military law and are tried in Israeli military courts (as well as in their own PA courts). Jews in the West Bank can vote in elections to the Knesset; Arabs cannot.

In 2017, a UN report concluded that "Israel has established an apartheid regime that dominates the Palestinian people as a whole"[16] and it is most "systematically practised by Israel in the West Bank," where their laws "intentionally serve the core purpose of racial domination."[17] The report enraged Israel and the United States, and the two states successfully pressured the UN to withdraw it.

Jerusalem

Since 1967, East Jerusalem has been regarded as part of Israel by the Israeli government. The vast majority of the Palestinians, who make up over 60 percent of the population, are defined as "permanent residents" and cannot vote in general elections. Residency rights entitle them to Israeli welfare benefits, and they can work and travel inside Israel.

However, residency rights can be revoked for betraying Israel's "trust," and houses are regularly demolished if built without the permits that are rarely granted. In 2019, 169 houses were demolished, forty-two of them by the owners, who would otherwise have had to pay for the demolition.[18] Jerusalem has been largely cut off from its West Bank hinterland since the Oslo Accords were signed. Its economy has shrunk, and Palestinians from the West Bank are required to obtain permits to visit the city.

Gaza

Before the events of October 7, 2023, Gaza was sometimes referred to as "the largest open-air prison" in the world.It remained under a tight Israeli blockade, while Egypt frequently closed its border with Gaza. It was dependent on Israel for most of its water and electricity. The lack of power hit businesses, hospitals, and sanitation facilities particularly hard, contributing to high levels of unemployment, ill health, and poverty. Sewage was sent, untreated, into the sea, and much tap water was undrinkable.

In 2020, 70 percent of the population was dependent on some form of humanitarian aid. In seeking to explain why she thought deprivation and despair led to suicide bombing and rocket fire, the *Haaretz* journalist Amira Hass, who lived in Gaza for several years before Israelis were banned from entering, wrote, "Let them breathe, and they will find out that life is more beautiful than death."[19]

Hamas's rule has been highly authoritarian, and since 2006, many Gazans have been executed for collaboration with the Israelis. Hamas's human rights abuses are widely resented in Gaza, yet many Gazans expressed pride in "the resistance."

Boycott, Divestment, Sanctions (BDS)

Nonviolent resistance to Israeli occupation has been maintained, not least by civil society initiatives such as the campaign for **Boycott, Divestment, Sanctions (BDS)**.

BDS is a campaign founded by over 170 Palestinian groups in 2005 to pressure Israel to recognise Palestinians rights. It does this by calling on public institutions and civic bodies to boycott, divest (withdraw investments) from, or impose sanctions on Israeli companies that produce goods in illegal settlements and on the foreign companies doing business with them. However, it champions the rights of all Palestinians, including those of Palestinian citizens of Israel and Palestinian refugees.

BDS is not based on a political program. Its struggle is for equal human rights and its chief strategy has been to build international solidarity. To this end, it has achieved considerable success in mobilizing support among trade unions, student bodies, churches, and other civic bodies across the world. In this way, it has acted as a lever to open and broaden discussion about the Palestinian predicament.

By focusing on Israel's treatment of its Palestinian citizens and of the Palestinians in the occupied territories, BDS has challenged Israel's image as a liberal, humane, and democratic country. By calling for equal, democratic rights for all people living between the Mediterranean and the Jordan River, it has challenged Israel's existence as a Jewish-majority state.

Israel has claimed that BDS aims to delegitimise Israel – it challenges Israel's right to exist and is therefore anti-Semitic. This has led Zeev Sternhell, an Israeli journalist, to criticise the West's political elite for "not speaking out openly against Israeli colonialism, for fear of encouraging the anti-Semitic monster" and to say that "at the universities and in the schools, in the media and on social networks [in the West], they are already saying explicitly: it is untenable that the Jewish past serve as a justification for cruelty in the Palestinian present."[20]

The Crisis of May 2021

In May 2021, violence erupted in East Jerusalem. It was triggered by the threatened eviction of Palestinian families from the Arab neighbourhood of Sheikh Jarrah and subsequent Palestinian protests. When confrontations between Palestinians and Israelis spread to the Old City, the Israeli police stormed the al-Aqsa Mosque. More than three hundred people were injured, mostly Palestinians.

Three days later, Hamas issued an ultimatum to Israel to withdraw its forces from the al-Aqsa Mosque compound. Later that day, Hamas and Islamic Jihad began firing rockets into Israel from Gaza, hitting residential areas and a school. Israel retaliated with a campaign of airstrikes against Gaza. The main targets were the offices and homes of Hamas leaders and the tunnels through which they moved weapons. However, in the eleven-day campaign, 278 Palestinians were killed in Gaza, 66 of them children. Hamas and Islamic Jihad fired nearly three

Palestinians inspect destruction caused by Israeli air strikes in the southern Gaza Strip, May 2021.

thousand rockets into Israel, killing thirteen Israelis, including two children. A ceasefire went into effect on May 21, 2021.

During Israel's campaign against Gaza, there were widespread protests and demonstrations across the West Bank and in Arab parts of Israel itself. The Israeli government was particularly surprised by the outbreak of protests by Palestinian citizens within Israel that demonstrated both solidarity with fellow Palestinians in the occupied territories and resentment at their own second-class status within Israel.

In April 2022, there was a spate of killings carried out by Palestinians within Israel. In response, Israel launched military raids across the West Bank. It was during one such raid, in the town of Jenin, in May 2022, that Shireen Abu Akleh, a prominent Palestinian-American journalist, was killed. After weeks of investigation, the UN concluded that she had been killed by Israeli forces and not by "indiscriminate firing by armed Palestinians, as initially claimed by Israeli authorities."

In the November 2022 elections, Netanyahu was ree-lected with the support of two extreme right-wing parties. The new government proposed to expand Israeli settle-ments, with some of its members calling for the annexa-tion of all or parts of the West Bank.

Less than a year later, on October 7, 2023, Hamas launched a surprise attack on Israel, firing a barrage of rockets from Gaza and sending fighters across the border. More than 1,200 Israelis and foreign nationals, mostly civilians, were killed and about 240, including foreign nationals, were taken hostage by Hamas and moved to Gaza. In retaliation, Israel began an aerial bombardment of Gaza and imposed a siege, cutting off supplies of food and water, fuel and medicines.

Three weeks later, Israel launched a ground offensive to destroy Hamas and free the hostages. As of 30 November, it was estimated that over 15,000 Palestinians had been killed, 40% of them children, and that over half of Gaza's population of 2.3 million people had been displaced within Gaza. Meanwhile, 235 Palestinians had been killed in the occupied West Bank, either by the Israeli army or by Israeli settlers.

In late November, the government of Qatar brokered a deal whereby Israeli hostages would be exchanged for Palestinians in Israeli prisons. It was agreed that both sides would observe a ceasefire and Israel would allow trucks carrying food, water and medicines into Gaza. For seven nights, such exchanges took place, and, by 30 November/ end of the month, 86 Israelis, 24 foreign nationals and 240 Palestinians had been released. Then, on 1 December, the truce broke down and fighting resumed.

At the time of writing, the future for both Israelis and Palestinians is more bleak and uncertain than ever.

Personal Testimony

In October 2018, the author, spent eight days in the West Bank under the auspices of the Israeli Committee Against House Demolitions (ICAHD), together with twenty other international volunteers. Below are extracts from my diary:

> We spent four days helping to build a community center in the village of Bardala, in the north of the Jordan Valley. The center of the village is in Area B (under Palestinian municipal control but overall Israeli military control) but the outskirts and neighboring villages are in Area C (under direct Israeli military rule). The community center is to serve as a meeting place for the inhabitants of several villages. None of these surrounding small villages in Area C has a school. There was one but it was demolished by the Israel Defense Forces (IDF) on the grounds that it had not been granted a permit. In Area C, which includes most of the Jordan Valley, no wells can be dug and no new structures built (house, school, or medical clinic) without the permission of the Israeli authorities, and, as UN statistics show, this is very rarely granted.
>
> Farming is the main source of livelihood

for the village of Bardala and it has rich, fertile agricultural land growing vegetables such as eggplants, tomatoes, and cucumbers. However, it depends on a reliable supply of water. The Jordan Valley has plentiful supplies of water, from the river and springs, but the Israelis have reduced the village's water supply and occasionally they cut it off completely. In fact, on September 17, a month before we arrived, Israeli forces had arrived with three military jeeps and two bulldozers. They cut off the water supply and proceeded to destroy 1,600 feet of water pipes that supply local farms, thus threatening the livelihood of fifty farmers.

In a very small village nearby, the community had had its water supply permanently cut off and was now forced to buy in tankers of water weekly and even that tanker had been impounded on occasion. The stream nearby had been polluted by sewage thrown down from the Israeli settlement above so that it was no longer fit for human or animal consumption.

One day we visited a farmer, in the village of Al-Hadidya, a Bedouin community. The village, which is surrounded by three military bases and three settlements, used to be home to fifty-four families; now only twelve families remain because of house demolitions. The farmer told us how he grazes sheep and goats. He is a local leader and, no doubt because he is an activist, his house had been destroyed many times: initially razed to the ground, then partially rebuilt by the family the next morning only to be destroyed yet again, and so on. He spoke with power, passion, and conviction, swearing that he would never leave his land. His daughter is called Sumud ("steadfastness"), which says it all.

On another occasion, five members of our group, accompanied by a rabbi from *Torat Tzedet* (Torah of Justice), went out in the morning with a shepherd and his goats. At one point, three members of the IDF, all young, appeared and accosted them. They asked what the group were doing and one said that they were protecting the shepherd from harassment by settlers from the hilltop, a comment which was met by sarcasm ("poor shepherd," etc.). The group was informed that they were in a "military firing zone" (56 percent of the Jordan Valley is categorized as closed military firing zone; little of it is used as such). Although the rabbi had a map to show that they were not doing so, the IDF disagreed. No doubt they were under orders to stop and interrogate the shepherd and his "protectors." The shepherd was detained for longer than the volunteers; two days earlier, when alone, he had been handcuffed and blindfolded while under interrogation. Fortunately, his goats had found their way home: otherwise, he might have lost his flock, either to dehydration or disorientation. The soldiers were no doubt told, and believed, that they were protecting outpost settlers and that the shepherd, under the influence of activists/internationals, was a threat to their security. A more likely explanation is that his arrest and interrogation was an example of the harassment and humiliation designed to deter the shepherd from using his customary grazing ground. The destruction of Palestinians' livelihood would appear to be a deliberate aim of both settlers and military.

Given the arrests, interrogations, demolitions, and lack of access to water and education referred to in this one small area and the fact that much of the most fertile land in the Jordan Valley was seized by the Israelis in 1967, for commercial use (70 percent of Israel's dates are produced here), it is not surprising that the Palestinian population in the valley has fallen, since 1967, from about three hundred thousand to below sixty thousand. Many of those left reside in Jericho, the one major city in the valley, so that perhaps only twenty thousand remain farming the land or grazing their herds. Many have migrated to Jordan and Syria and are now refugees, never allowed to return.

We spent four days harvesting olives in the village of Burin, near Nablus. We actually stayed in the nearby village of Awarta in the house of Aziz [not his real name], an olive farmer, who had, in the past, been attacked by settlers and, on one occasion, been terrified into fleeing with his son while their tractor was torched. We picked olives on land just below a settlement, owned by a family who are now too afraid to harvest their olives because they have been harassed by armed settlers so often. We took it in turns to be on "guard duty." There are 120 "outposts," which are unofficial and not recognized by the Israeli government. Settlers residing in these outposts are often young and armed and, invariably, soldiers are posted nearby. Furthermore, evidence shows that such outposts are connected to the electricity grid and to water supplies and are retrospectively authorized.

On one day when it was too windy to pick olives, we visited Nablus. Our guide for the day was Hamid, a farmer who had experienced several spells of administrative detention (with neither charge nor trial), totaling five years in all over the course of a decade. Why? he was asked. He replied that he had been told by his captors that he was "a troublemaker." He's articulate, an activist within his community, a village leader. His father had spent fourteen years in Israeli jails and both his mother and his brother had done time too. The Israelis' aim? To break our will to resist, he replied.

We were all shocked by the many different forms of harassment, by both settlers and

IDF, which we witnessed in the course of just eight days. We also saw many examples of resilience, of *sumud*, in the face of the ongoing trauma that is life under occupation. Many remain determined to stay on their land and not give up. It is both inspiring and humbling. However, increasing displacement, particularly from Area C, attests to the success of a policy that several writers, including Israelis, have described as ethnic cleansing, even if most Israelis describe it as Judaization.

Postscript

On August 29, 2019, Israeli troops and the Israeli water company, Mekorot, severed water pipes that were used to irrigate fields in Bardala. Some weeks later, they also cut pipes and demolished a water reservoir in the same village.[21]

On June 8, 2021, Israeli soldiers entered the village and demolished two water reservoirs, used for farming, that had been donated by the EU.[22] On June 29, 2021, Israeli soldiers removed a tent that settlers had erected on the land of a Palestinian farmer from Burin. In response, settlers set fire to olive trees in the village. The soldiers prevented a Palestinian fire truck from arriving and putting out the fire. When the fire reached the access road to the settlement, an Israeli fire truck was called to prevent the fire from spreading toward the settlement. Over 1,200 olive trees were damaged.[23]

Epilogue

At the time of writing, the politics of Israel-Palestine are being transformed following the events of October 7, 2023. Israel lost more lives in a single day than in all the wars of 1956, 1967 and 1973 combined. Then followed weeks of bombardment and fighting and the displacement, within Gaza, of 1.5 million people. At the time of going to press, Israel is only allowing very limited supplies of water, food, fuel electricity to be delivered and Gaza faces a humanitarian disaster. The sheer scale, and the lasting impact, of this crisis is hard to comprehend.

All the narratives analyzed in this book remain key to understanding future prospects for the region. Furthermore, such understanding is essential for any resolution of the conflict. The range of responses which this crisis has evoked around the world demonstrates the urgent need for a better understanding of the past in order to craft a better future. The outcomes are unknown and unknowable and it is difficult to write about events that are happening in real time.

The reconstruction of Gaza and the prospects for peace

Much of Gaza has been physically destroyed and over 1.5 million people have been displaced and made homeless. At the time of writing, Gaza is on the brink of a humanitarian catastrophe and the outbreak of contagious disease is highly likely. Even if starvation is avoided, the people of Gaza will experience hardship for years to come.

When the fighting is over, the UN is the body best-equipped to feed and to provide shelter and healthcare for the people of Gaza. The UN is also probably the body that should oversee reconstruction but who will pay?

Who will be responsible for the security of the Gaza Strip, both to protect the thousands of aid workers who will be required as well as the people of Gaza? The Israelis, trau-matised by Hamas' atrocities and fearful of future attacks launched from Gaza, have stated their intention to oversee security. The US government disagrees and has suggested that the Palestinian Authority (PA) should govern Gaza. However, In the West Bank today, the PA has lost credibility with many Palestinians. It faces widespread criticism for its continued cooperation with the Israeli military.

Although US support is vital for any new international initiative for longer-term peace-making, the US is no longer seen by the Palestinians as an honest broker. There needs to be an international peace-keeping force, preferably under a UN and Arab League mandate, to ensure that the recon-struction of Gaza takes place and that Palestinians' fear of an ongoing Nakba, of being forced to move out of Gaza, is not realised. Most of Gaza's residents have been refugees since 1948.

And how is the wider Israel-Palestine conflict to be resolved so that endless rounds of fighting are avoided in the future? A just and lasting peace first requires that the equal rights of Palestinians, particularly their right to self-determination, as acknowledged by the UN, are recognised by all states. Most states have recognised Palestine. The US, the UK and many European countries have yet to do so.

A new international initiative must be rooted in international law, reuniting Gaza with the rest of the Occupied Palestinian Territory. Palestinians, both from Gaza and the West Bank, will have to be involved in both reconstruction and peace-making. It is not for others to determine how Palestinians are to be governed and who they choose to lead them. The Palestinians of Gaza, the West Bank and East Jerusalem should hold elections to determine how they wish to be governed.

The future for Israel

No one knows who will be governing Israel in the future. The political and military leadership acknowledge that there will have to be a reckoning to explain the failure of their intelligence and the slowness of the military response in Israel on October 7. The Israelis are likely to face a general election in the not-too-distant future to decide how they too wish to be governed.

Whether Israel manages to eliminate Hamas as a military force or not, the idea and identity of Hamas is unlikely to be destroyed. In fact, the more destruction and destitution wrought by Israel in Gaza, the more likely it is that future generations will be radicalised. Nevertheless, any resolution of the conflict will need to take account of the traumatic impact on Israelis of the Hamas' attack of October 2023. It will have a long-lasting psychological effect. At the time of writing, 250,000 Israelis are internally displaced from near the Gaza border and from northern Israel, the latter as a result of attacks by Hezbollah from Lebanon. Many in Israel will continue to fear that any relaxation of their control over the occupied territories will lead to another violent intifada or cross-border assault.

Similarly, for Palestinians to be able to live in peace and security, the actions of extremist Jewish settlers to force Palestinians from their homes and lands in the West Bank must be stopped and the Government of Israel must be required to curb these criminal actions.

In recent decades, the stronger party in the conflict, Israel, has had little incentive to negotiate: its economy is strong, it has the constant support of the US government and its increasing colonization of Palestinian land has been subject to only muted international condemnation. Furthermore, there has been little domestic pressure to enter negotiations and may be even less after Hamas' attack.

It will require sustained pressure from the international community to persuade the Israeli government that its own interests are best served by reaching a resolution based on the implementation of international law. The powers with the greatest diplomatic and economic leverage are the United States, the EU, and Britain. As stated earlier, the recognition of Palestine by those states that have not yet done so would constitute an acknowledgement of the Palestinians' right to national self-determination. Such moves could have a significant impact on Israeli policy.

Neighbours not enemies?

It may be many years before a majority of Israelis conclude that a resolution of their conflict with the Palestinians, with whom they share the land, would be a better way to ensure their long-term security.

A peace based on the Palestinians' right to self-determination and equal rights would end the financial and morally corrosive cost of conscripting young Israeli men and women to enforce the occupation. A settlement based on international law would enable Israel to establish full diplomatic relations with most of the Arab world and end the growing perception of Israel as an apartheid and undemocratic state.

Palestinians and Israelis will always be neighbours. As Yitzhak Rabin, the former Israeli Prime Minister, said: Israelis and Palestinians are 'destined to live together on the same soil, in the same land'. An agreement based on equality and justice could enable both to live in peace and security.

Notes

1. The Origins of the Conflict

1. Figures taken from James Gelvin, *The Israel-Palestine Conflict: One Hundred Years of War* (New York: Cambridge University Press, 2007), p. 25.

2. Quoted in Benny Morris, *Righteous Victims: A History of the Zionist-Arab Conflict, 1881–1999* (London: John Murray, 1999), p. 23.

3. Zion is a biblical name for the mountain outside Jerusalem, often used to describe the biblical land of Israel as a whole.

4. Quoted in Morris, *Righteous Victims*, p. 342.

5. Quoted in Ian Black, *Enemies and Neighbours: Arabs and Jews in Palestine and Israel, 1917–2017* (London: Allen Lane, 2017), p. 26.

6. Ari Shavit, *My Promised Land: The Triumph and Tragedy of Israel* (London: Scribe, 2014), pp. 12–13.

2. The First World War and the British Mandate

1. Lord Curzon, who became foreign secretary in 1919, was quite certain that "we gave him [Hussein] the assurance that Palestine . . . should be Arab and independent."

2. Christian Zionism is a belief among some Christians that the return of the Jews to the Holy Land is in accordance with Bible prophecy.

3. Quoted in Charles Smith, *Palestine and the Arab-Israeli Conflict* (Boston: Bedford/St Martin's, 2007), p. 8.

4. Sir Martin Gilbert, Irene and Hyman Kreitman Annual Lecture: "Sowing the seeds of Jewish statehood: Britain and Palestine, 1909–22," Ben Gurion University of the Negev, May 2011, youtube.com/watch?v=kub6d-ik6w (accessed April 27, 2019).

5. Quoted in Morris, *Righteous Victims*, p. 99.

6. Quoted in Tom Segev, *One Palestine, Complete* (London: Abacus, 2000), p. 141.

7. Quoted in Morris, *Righteous Victims*, p. 103.

8. Quoted in Segev, *One Palestine, Complete*, p. 116.

9. Joseph Baratz, *A Village by the Jordan* (London: Harvill Press, 1954), p. 13.

10. Deborah Bernstein and Musia Lipman, "Fragments of Life: From the Diaries of Two Young Women" in Deborah Bernstein (ed.), *Pioneers and Homemakers: Jewish Women in Pre-State Israel* (New York: State University of New York, 1992), p. 157.

11. Palestine Arab Delegation, "Observations on the High Commissioner's Interim Report on the Civil Administration of Palestine during the Period 1st July 1920–30th June 1921."

12. George Antonius, *The Arab Awakening* (New York: J. B. Lippincott, 1939), p. 391.

3. British Rule in Palestine, 1929–39

1. Rashid Khalidi, *The Iron Cage: The Story of the Palestinian Struggle for Statehood* (London: Oneworld Publications, 2015), p. 31.

2. Quoted in Black, *Enemies and Neighbours*, p. 39.

3. The tomb is believed by both Jews and Muslims to be the resting place of the biblical figures Abraham, his wife Sarah, Abraham's son Isaac, and his wife Rebekah.

4. Quoted in Black, *Enemies and Neighbours*, p. 63.

5. Quoted in Smith, *Palestine and the Arab-Israeli Conflict*, p. 161.

6. Quoted in Avi Shlaim, *The Iron Wall: Israel and the Arab World* (London: Penguin, 2000), p. 21.

7. Quoted in Morris, *Righteous Victims*, p. 140.

8. During the Second World War, Haj Amin met Hitler to enlist his support to end British rule, a move that associated the Palestinian national movement with anti-Semitism.

9. Rashid Khalidi, "The Palestinians and 1948: the underlying causes of failure" in Eugene Rogan and Avi Shlaim (eds.), *The War for Palestine* (Cambridge, UK: Cambridge University Press, 2001), p. 27.

10. Quoted in T. G. Fraser, *The Middle East 1914–1979* (London: Edward Arnold, 1980), pp. 23–4.

11. Quoted in Gudrun Krämer, *A History of Palestine* (Princeton, NJ: Princeton University Press, 2011), p. 294.

12. From the *Daily Mail*, 30 August 1939.

13. From Y. Porath, *The Emergence of the Palestinian-Arab Nationalist Movement, 1918–1929* (London: Frank Cass, 1974).

14. From E. C. Hodgkin (ed.), *Letters from Palestine, 1932–36* (London: Quartet Books, 1986), p. 160.

4. UN Partition, Israel, and War, 1945–49

1. Quoted in Ritchie Ovendale, *The Origins of the Arab-Israeli Wars* (Harlow: Pearson, 1999), p. 114.

2. Quoted in Michael Scott-Baumann, *The Middle East, 1908–2011* (London: Hodder Education, 2016), p. 26.

3. Menachem Begin, *The Revolt* (New York: Nash, 1951), p. 433.

4. Quoted in Black, *Enemies and Neighbours*, p. 109.

5. Ilan Pappe, *A History of Modern Palestine* (Cambridge, UK: Cambridge University Press, 2004), p. 136.

6. Begin, *The Revolt*, p. 164.

7. Benny Morris, *The Birth of the Palestinian Refugee Problem* (Cambridge, UK: Cambridge University Press, 1988).

8. Ilan Pappe, *The Ethnic Cleansing of Palestine* (Oxford, UK: Oneworld, 2007).

9. Pappe, *A History of Modern Palestine*, p. 130.

10. Morris, *The Birth of the Palestinian Refugee Problem*, p. 48.

11. Morris, *Righteous Victims*, p. 245.

12. Quoted in Black, *Enemies and Neighbours*, p. 128.

13. Quoted in Avi Shlaim, *The Iron Wall*, p. 40.

14. Chaim Herzog, *The Arab-Israeli Wars: War and Peace in the Middle East* (London: Arms and Armour Press, 1982), pp. 106–7.

15. Begin, *The Revolt*, pp. 164–5.

16. Mordecai Bar-On, "Remembering 1948" in Benny Morris (ed.), *Making Israel* (Michigan: University of Michigan Press, 2007), pp. 33–4.

17. Dina Matar, *What It Means to Be Palestinian: Stories of Palestinian Statehood* (London: IB Taurus, 2011), pp. 42–3.

5. Palestinians and Israelis, 1950s–60s

1. Ghazi Daniel, a Palestinian refugee, in an account published by the PLO Research Centre in 1972, quoted in "Arab-Israeli Conflict," Schools Council History 13–16 Project, p. 65.

2. Quoted in Donald Macintyre, *Gaza: Preparing for Dawn* (London: Oneworld, 2017), p. 10.

3. Quoted in Michael Scott-Baumann, *Conflict in the Middle East* (London: Hodder Education, 2007) p. 35.

4. Quoted in Helena Cobban, *The Palestinian Liberation Organisation: People, Power and Politics* (Cambridge, UK: Cambridge University Press, 1984), p. 21.

5. A phrase used by Rashid Khalidi, *The Iron Cage*, p. 141.

6. Abu Iyad, a Fatah leader, quoted in Rosemary Sayigh, *Palestinians: From Peasants to Revolutionaries* (London: Zed Books, 2013), p. 151.

7. Quoted in Cobban, *The Palestine Liberation Organisation*, p. 25.

8. Dina Matar, *What It Means to Be Palestinian*, p. 16.

9. Ari Shavit, *My Promised Land*, p. 267.

6. The Israeli Occupation of the Palestinian Territories

1. Quoted in Black, *Enemies and Neighbours*, p. 180.

2. The Israeli geovernment does not regard the Israelis there to be settlers nor does it consider the new neighbourhoods to be settlements.

3. Quoted in Neve Gordon, *Israel's Occupation* (London: University of California Press, 2008), p. 49.

4. Tom Segev, *1967: Israel, the War and the Year That Transformed the Middle East* (London: Little, Brown, 2007), p. 558.

5. An international treaty of 1907.

6. Article 49 of the Fourth Geneva Convention.

7. Gordon, *Israel's Occupation*, p. 118.

8. *Sabra* is a tough-skinned fruit to which the young, hardy generation of Jews in Palestine in the interwar years was likened.

9. Ronald Ranta, "Wasted Decade: Israel's Policies towards the Occupied Territories, 1967–1977," unpublished PhD thesis (University College, London), p. 98.

10. The Hague Convention allows an army to requisition land if "demanded by the necessities of war," as long as it is "temporary."

11. David Grossman, *The Yellow Wind*. Translated from Hebrew by Haim Watzman (London: Penguin, 2016), pp. 21–3.

12. Grossman, *The Yellow Wind*, pp. 34–5.

7. Palestinian Resistance and the First Intifada, 1967–87

1. Quoted in "Arab-Israeli Conflict," Schools Council History 13–16 Project, p. 65.

2. The term increasingly used by Fatah from 1967 to describe their movement.

3. The figures are disputed. Cobban quotes an Israeli journalist's estimate of two hundred as the number killed, Yezid Sayigh gives a figure nearer fifty.

4. Yezid Sayigh, *Armed Struggle and the Search for State: The Palestinian National Movement, 1949–1993* (Oxford: OUP, 1997), p. 179.

5. Interview in *Der Stern*, 16 September 1970.

6. Interview quoted in Walter Oppenheim, *The Middle East* (Simon & Schuster Education, 1989), p. 37.

7. Quoted in Fraser, *The Middle East 1914–1979*, p. 136.

8. Penny Johnson, "The West Bank Rises Up" in Zachary Lockman and Joel Beinin (eds.), *Intifada: The Palestinian Uprising Against Israeli Occupation* (Boston: South End Press, 1989), p. 30.

9. Quoted in Morris, *Righteous Victims*, p. 589.

10. Gordon, *Israel's Occupation*, p. 182.

11. Matar, *What It Means to Be Palestinian*, pp. 170–2.

8. The Rise and Demise of the Oslo Peace Process, 1993–2000

1. The PLO had moved their headquarters to Tunis after the Israeli invasion of Lebanon in 1982.

2. Quoted in Gilbert Achcar, *Eastern Cauldron: Islam, Afghanistan, Palestine and Iraq in a Marxist Mirror* (London: Pluto Press, 2004), p. 214.

3. Sari Nusseibeh, *Once Upon a Country: A Palestinian Life* (London: Halban, 2007), p. 374.

4. Quoted in Gordon, *Israel's Occupation*, p. 189.

5. Quoted in Adam Hanieh, *The Oslo Illusion*, p. 2, jacobinmag.com/2013/04/the-oslo-illusion.

6. Quoted in Baruch Kimmerling and Joel Migdal, *The Palestinian People: A History* (London: Harvard University Press, 2003), p. 335.

7. The figure is quoted in Khalil Shikaki, "The Peace Process, National Reconstruction, and the Transition to Democracy in Palestine," *Journal of Palestine Studies* 25, no. 2 (2005), pp. 5–20.

8. Edward Said, *The End of the Peace Process: Oslo and After* (London: Granta Books, 2000), p. 6.

9. Meron Benvenisti, *Intimate Enemies: Jews and Arabs in a Shared Land* (London: University of California Press, 1995), p. 206.

10. Benvenisti, *Intimate Enemies*, p. 218.

11. Khalidi, *The Iron Cage*, p. 197.

12. Dan Rabinowitz, "Belated Occupation, Advanced Militarization: Edward Said's critique of the Oslo Process Revisited," *Critical Inquiry* 31, no. 2 (2005), pp. 505–11.

13. Figures taken from Arnie Arnon, "Israeli policy towards the Occupied Palestinian Territories: The Economic Dimension, 1967–2007," *Middle East Journal* 61, no. 4 (2007), p. 588.

14. Adam Hanieh, *Lineages of Revolt: Issues of Contemporary Capitalism in the Middle East* (London: Haymarket Books, 2013), p. 109.

15. Leila Farsakh, "From Domination to Destruction: The Palestinian Economy under the Israeli Occupation" in Adi Ophir, Michal Givoni and Sari Hanafi (eds.), *The Power of Inclusive Exclusion: The Anatomy of Israeli Rule in the Occupied Palestinian Territories* (New York: Zone Books, 2009), p. 390.

16. IMF figures quoted in Nusseibeh, *Once Upon a Country*, p. 401.

17. Figures from Leila Farsakh, *Palestinian Labour Migration to Israel: Labour, Land and Occupation* (Abingdon: Routledge, 2005), p. 395.

18. Quoted in Black, *Enemies and Neighbours*, p. 356.

19. Quoted in Graham Usher, *Dispatches from Palestine: The Rise and Fall of the Oslo Peace Process* (London: Pluto Press, 1999), p. 74.

20. From an interview with the author, Usher, p. 145.

21. Quoted in Black, *Enemies and Neighbours*, p. 359.

22. Gelvin, *The Israel–Palestine Conflict*, p. 241.

23. Quoted in Ahron Bregman, *Cursed Victory: A History of Israel and the Occupied Territories* (London: Penguin, 2015), p. 242.

24. Shlaim, *Israel and Palestine: Reappraisals, Revision, Refutations* (London: Verso, 2009), p. 205.

25. Shlaim, *Israel and Palestine*, p. 208.

26. Shavit, *My Promised Land*, pp. 258–60.

27. Nusseibeh, *Once Upon a Country*, p. 395.

28. Shapira, *Israel: A History*, pp. 443–44.

9. From the Second Intifada to War in Gaza, 2000–08

1. Oren Yiftachel, *Ethnocracy: Land and Identity Politics in Israel/ Palestine* (Philadelphia: University of Pennsylvania Press, 2006), p. 76.

2. Nusseibeh, *Once Upon a Country*, p. 399.

3. Shlaim, *Israel and Palestine*, p. 285.

4. Baruch Kimmerling, *Politicide: Ariel Sharon's War Against the Palestinians* (London: Verso, 2003), pp. 161–2.

5. Quoted in Bregman, *Cursed Victory*, p. 270.

6. Susan Nathan, *The Other Side of Israel: My Journey Across the Jewish-Arab Divide* (London: Harper, 2006), p. 67.

7. Quoted in Bregman, *Cursed Victory*, pp. 291–2.

8. Quoted in Bregman, *Cursed Victory*, p. 295.

9. Quoted in Shlaim, *Israel and Palestine*, p. 294.

10. Quoted in Gelvin, *The Israel–Palestine Conflict*, p. 250.

11. Quoted in Gregory Harms and Todd Ferry, *The Palestinian-Israeli Conflict* (London: Pluto, 2017), p. 184.

12. Shlaim, *The Iron Wall*, p. 689.

13. Quoted in Tareq Baconi, *Hamas Contained* (Stanford, CA: Stanford University Press, 2018), p. 35.

14. Harry S. Truman Research Institute for the Advancement of Peace at the Hebrew University of Jerusalem and the Palestinian Centre for Policy and Survey Research in Ramallah, September 2006.

15. Quoted in Macintyre, *Gaza: Preparing for Dawn*, p. 107.

16. Quoted in Baconi, *Hamas Contained*, p. 125.

17. Quoted in Dov Waxman, *The Palestinian-Israeli Conflict: What Everyone Needs to Know* (Oxford, UK: Oxford University Press, 2019), p. 140.

18. Some put the number much higher, e.g., Colin Shindler, *A History of Modern Israel* (Cambridge, UK: Cambridge University Press, 2013), p. 374.

19. WHO figures quoted in Black, *Enemies and Neighbours*, p. 426.

20. Quoted in Shlaim, *The Iron Wall*, p. 803. Goldstone later retracted his charge against Israel, but other members of the UN commission did not.

21. Philip Winslow, *Victory for Us Is to See You Suffer*, (Boston: Beacon Press, 2007) pp. 81–2.

22. Shavit, *My Promised Land*, p. 331.

23. Raja Shehadeh, *Palestinian Walks* (London: Profile Books, 2007), pp. 183 and 185.

10. Palestinians and Israelis in the Age of Netanyahu, 2009–PRESENT

1. Avi Shlaim, writing in *The Iron Wall*, believed there was as much as 90 percent support, p. 804.

2. According to Shlaim, *The Iron Wall*, p. 807.

3. Gershon Shafir, *A Half-Century of Occupation: Israel, Palestine and the World's Most Intractable Problem* (California: University of California Press, 2017), p. 98.

4. *Independent*, 29 April 2014.

5. Waxman, *The Israeli-Palestinian Conflict*, p. 199, quoting from a classified US diplomatic cable from 2008 that was published by Wikileaks.

6. Quoted in Waxman, *The Israeli-Palestinian Conflict*, p. 208.

7. *Times of Israel*, 29 July 2014, quoted in Black, *Enemies and Neighbours*, p. 453.

8. Quoted in Black, *Enemies and Neighbours*, p. 468.

9. Quoted in the *The Independent*, May 3, 2014, when the legislation was introduced.

10. Quoted in Black, *Enemies and Neighbours*, p. 472.

11. Reported in *The Times*, December 17, 2016.

12. Quoted in Ghada Karmi, "Constantly Dangled, Endlessly Receding," *London Review of Books* 41, no. 23 (2019).

13. *Haaretz*, January 30, 2020.

14. Nur Masalha, quoted in Oren Yiftachel, *Ethnocracy: Land and Identity Politics in Israel/Palestine*, p. 64.

15. Raja Shehadeh, *Language of War, Language of Peace: Palestine, Israel and the Search for Justice* (London: Profile Books, 2015), p. 91.

16. Although the term "apartheid" was originally associated with the system of white minority rule in South Africa, it now represents a crime against humanity under international law.

17. UN Report 2017, "Israeli Practices towards the Palestinian People and the Question of Apartheid."

18. B'Tselem website (accessed March 21, 2020): btselem.org/ planning_and_building/east_jerusalem_statistics.

19. Quoted in Shehadeh, *Language of War*, p. 111.

20. Quoted in Shehadeh, *Language of War*, p. 126.

21. Jordan Valley Solidarity website (accessed April 7, 2020): jordanvalleysolidarity .org/news/army-mekorot-destroy- palestinian-wells-bardala.

22. The Israeli Committee Against House Demolitions (ICAHD) website (accessed July 20, 2021): icahd.de/sagt-nicht-ihr-haettet-es-nicht-gewusst-747.

23. ICAHD website (accessed July 20, 2021): icahd.de/sagt-nicht-ihr-haettet-es-nicht-gewusst-nr-752.

Glossary of Key Terms

aliyah: A wave of Jewish immigration to Palestine; Hebrew for "ascent"

annex: To add to one's territory, usually by force

anti-Semitism: Prejudice or hatred toward Jews

apartheid: Literally, "separate development," usually referring to white-dominated South Africa before 1990 where a system of laws enforced territorial and political separation between Black and white South Africans

Arab Higher Committee (AHC): Council established by leading Arab notables in 1936

Arab League: Established in 1945 to represent the Arab states

Ashkenazi Jews: Jews from Central or Eastern Europe

Balfour Declaration: Statement issued by the British Government in 1917 promising support for a Jewish homeland in Palestine

Boycott, Divestment, Sanctions (BDS): Movement founded by Palestinians to pressurise Israel to recognise Palestinian rights

B'Tselem: The Israeli Information Center for Human Rights in the Occupied Territories. It documents human rights violations by Israel in the occupied territories.

"Conquest of Labor": The concept of calling on Jews to hire Jewish, rather than non-Jewish, labour

"Conquest of Land": A concept emphasizing the need to colonise the land of Palestine

Cold War: The state of tension between the United States and the Soviet Union from the late 1940s to the late 1980s

***Eretz* Israel:** The ancient Hebrew term for the biblical "Land of Israel"

Evangelical Christians: Christians who believe that Christ's second coming will only occur when all Jews have returned to the "Land of Israel"

Fatah: Palestinian guerrilla group founded by Yasser Arafat

fedayeen: Literally, "those who sacrifice themselves," Palestinians who carried out raids on Israel

***Filastin*:** The Arabic for Palestine. The word "Palestine" derives from *Philistia*, the name given by Greek writers to the land of the Philistines, who lived in the south of what is today Israel in the twelfth century BCE.

Green Line: The pre-1967 boundary between Israel and the West Bank

Gush Emunim (Bloc of the Faithful): An organisation of Jewish religious nationalists formed to advance settlement building in the occupied territories

Haganah: Jewish military force, later to form the basis of the Israel Defense Forces (IDF)

Hamas: Acronym for "Islamic Resistance Movement"; a Palestinian movement founded in Gaza during the Second Intifada. It opposed the Oslo Accords.

Histadrut: Jewish trade union federation

intifada: Literally, "shaking off" in Arabic, the term is used to refer to the Palestinian uprisings that started in 1987 and 2000.

Irgun: Military group formed by the Revisionist followers of Vladimir Jabotinsky

Islamic Jihad: Palestinian Islamic group that calls for the establishment of an Islamic state in Palestine

Israel Defense Forces (IDF): The Israeli armed forces

Israeli Labor Party: A party built on the foundations of the Mapai (see page 254), which had been formed in 1930s Palestine

Jewish Agency: The governing body of the Zionist movement in Palestine during the British Mandate

Jewish National Fund (JNF): A body founded in 1901 to buy land for the Jewish community in Palestine. It still funds settlement building in the West Bank.

keffiyeh: Traditional Arab headdress

kibbutzim: Collective agricultural communities established by the Zionists

Knesset: The Israeli Parliament

Law of Return: Israeli law passed in 1950, which grants all Jews the right to Israeli citizenship

Likud Party: The right-wing Israeli party founded in 1973, which advocated increased settlement building. Led by Menachem Begin, it became the largest party in the Knesset in 1977.

mandate: A system devised by the League of Nations whereby Britain and France were made responsible for the government of the Arab lands of the former Ottoman Empire

Mapai: Political party founded by David Ben-Gurion in 1930, later to form the basis of the Israeli Labor Party

Mizrahi Jews: Jews who immigrated to Israel from Arab lands after 1948

Nakba: Arabic word for "disaster" or "catastrophe," used to refer to the war of 1948–49 and the refugee problem that resulted

Occupied Palestinian Territories (OPTs): The territories (West Bank, Gaza, and East Jerusalem) occupied by Israeli troops since 1967

Oslo Accords: Agreements reached between Israel and the Palestinians in 1993 and 1995

Ottomans: The Turkish dynasty, named after its founder, Osman, which ruled Palestine and other Arab lands up to 1918

Palestine Legislative Council (PLC): The Palestinian legislative body elected by Palestinians living in the occupied territories

Palestine Liberation Organisation (PLO): Set up in 1964 to lead the struggle to regain Palestine

Palestinian Authority (PA): A Palestinian "government," with limited authority, established as a result of the Oslo Accord in 1993 (for the administration of those areas of the West Bank and Gaza not under direct Israeli rule)

Peace Now: An Israeli movement that opposes continued settlement building and advocates a two-state resolution of the conflict

Quartet: The United States, European Union, United Nations, and Russia; all four declared their support for the "Roadmap for Peace" in 2003.

Revisionist Party: Militant Zionist party founded by Vladimir Jabotinsky

right of return: The right, claimed by many Palestinians, to return to their homes inside the Green Line, which they left during the *Nakba* in 1948

sabra: The cactus, native to Palestine, to which young Zionists working on the land were likened

Sephardic Jews: Originally Jews from Spain, but, more commonly now, Jews coming to Israel from Arab countries

Six-Day War: The 1967 war in which Israel defeated Egypt, Syria, and Jordan and occupied the West Bank and Gaza

Stern Gang: Zionist terrorist group founded in 1939

sumud: Arabic for "steadfastness," staying put, clinging on

Supreme Muslim Council (SMC): A body established by the British to administer Islamic schools, courts, etc.

Unified National Leadership of the Uprising (UNLU): A Palestinian body that emerged in 1988 to coordinate the strikes and demonstrations during the First Intifada

United Nations Relief and Works Agency (UNRWA): Agency set up by the United Nations to administer Palestinian refugee camps

West Bank: The Palestinian land on the west bank of the Jordan River, occupied by Israel since 1967

World Zionist Organization (WZO): Formed in 1897 to advocate for a secure homeland for Jews in Palestine

Yishuv: Hebrew for "settlement," referring to the Jewish community in Palestine during the mandate years

Zionism: The belief that the Jews represent a national community and are entitled to their own independent state

Glossary of Key People

Abbas, Mahmoud (1935–): Head of PLO delegation to Oslo; elected chairman of the PLO and president of the PA on Arafat's death in 2004

Abdullah (1882–1951): King of Transjordan

Arafat, Yasser (1929–2004): Founder of Fatah in 1959 and chairman of the PLO 1969–2004; signed the Oslo Accords with Yitzhak Rabin and was later elected president of the PA

Balfour, Arthur (1848–1930): The British foreign secretary who issued the declaration of support for a Jewish homeland

Barak, Ehud (1942–): Israeli general and prime minister 1999–2001

Begin, Menachem (1913–92): Leader of Irgun 1943–48; leader of Likud Party and prime minister of Israel 1977–83

Ben-Gurion, David (1886–1973): Emigrated from Poland to Palestine in 1906; became leader of the Jewish Agency in Palestine, founder of Mapai (later the Israeli Labor Party) in 1930 and first prime minister of Israel

Dayan, Moshe (1915–81): Israeli general and defence minister during the Six-Day War

Herzl, Theodor (1860–1904): Viennese journalist and author of *The Jewish State* (1896) who organised First Zionist Congress in 1897

Hussein, King of Jordan (1935–99): Succeeded his grandfather Abdullah as king in 1953 and expelled the PLO from Jordan in 1970

Hussein, Sharif of Mecca (1852–1931): Guardian of the holy sites of Mecca and Medina; agreed to raise an Arab army to fight against the Turks after being promised independence for the Arabs

al-Husseini, Haj Amin (1897–1974): Head of a prominent notable family, Grand Mufti of Jerusalem; head of the Supreme Muslim Council and leader of the Arab Higher Committee from 1936

Jabotinsky, Vladimir (1880–1940): Emigrated to Palestine from Russia and founded the Revisionist Party in 1925; an advocate of an "iron wall" of Zionist military force

Nasser, Gamal Abdel (1918–70): President of Egypt 1954–70

Nashashibis: Notable Jerusalem family, rivals to the Husseinis

Netanyahu, Benjamin (1949–): Prime minister of the Likud-led Israeli government 1996–99 and 2009–2021

Nusseibeh, Sari (1949–): Palestinian academic and former president of Al-Quds University in Jerusalem

Obama, Barack (1961–): US president 2009–17

Peres, Shimon (1923–2014): Defence and foreign minister at different times, as well as prime minister three times and president of Israel 2007–14

al-Qassam, Izz ad-Din (1882–1935): Popular Muslim preacher who fought against the British in Palestine; killed by the British, he became a symbol of popular resistance for Palestinians

Rabin, Yitzhak (1922–95): Israeli general, politician, and prime minister from 1974–77 and again from 1992–95. He signed the Oslo Accords with Yasser Arafat.

Samuel, Sir Herbert (1870–1963): High commissioner to Palestine (1920–25) during the British Mandate

Sharon, Ariel (1926–2014): Israeli general and politician, who was prime minister from 2001–06; chief architect of the settlement program

Trump, Donald (1946–): US president 2017–21 and author of the "Deal of the Century" in 2020

Weizmann, Chaim (1874–1952): Championed the Zionist cause in the UK at the time of the Balfour Declaration, head of World Zionist Organization from 1920, and first president of Israel

Bibliography

Books

Achcar, Gilbert, *Eastern Cauldron: Islam, Afghanistan, Palestine and Iraq in a Marxist Mirror* (London: Pluto Press, 2004).

Antonius, George, *The Arab Awakening* (New York: J. B. Lippincott, 1939).

Aronson, Geoffrey, *Israel, Palestinians and the Intifada: Creating Facts on the West Bank* (London: Kegan Paul International, 1990).

Baconi, Tareq, *Hamas Contained* (Stanford, CA: Stanford University Press, 2018).

Baratz, Joseph, *A Village by the Jordan* (London: Harvill Press, 1954).

Bauck, Peter and Omer, Mohammed (eds.), *The Oslo Accords: A Critical Assessment* (New York: American University of Cairo Press, 2016).

Begin, Menachem, *The Revolt* (New York: Nash, 1951).

Beilin,Yossi, *Touching Peace: From the Oslo Accord to a Final Agreement.* Translated from Hebrew by Philip Simpson (London: Weidenfeld and Nicholson, 1999).

Benvenisti, Meron, *Intimate Enemies: Jews and Arabs in a Shared Land* (London: University of California Press, 1995).

Bernstein, Deborah (ed.), *Pioneers and Homemakers: Jewish Women in Pre-State Israel* (New York: State University of New York, 1992).

Black, Ian, *Enemies and Neighbours: Arabs and Jews in Palestine and Israel, 1917–2017* (London: Allen Lane, 2017).

Bregman, Ahron, *Cursed Victory: A History of Israel and the Occupied Territories* (London: Penguin, 2015).

Cobban, Helena, *The Palestine Liberation Organisation: People, Power and Politics* (Cambridge, UK: Cambridge University Press, 1984).

Falk, Richard, *Palestine's Horizon Towards a Just Peace* (London: Pluto Press, 2017).

Farsakh, Leila, *Palestinian Labour Migration to Israel: Labour, Land and Occupation* (Abingdon: Routledge, 2005).

Fraser, T. G., *The Middle East 1914–1979* (London: Edward Arnold, 1980).

Gelvin, James, *The Israel-Palestine Conflict: One Hundred Years of War* (New York: Cambridge University Press, 2007).

Giacaman, George and Lonning, Dag (eds.), *After Oslo, New Realities, Old Problems* (London: Pluto Press, 1998).

Gordon, Neve, *Israel's Occupation* (London: University of California Press, 2008).

Grossman, David, *The Yellow Wind*. Translated from Hebrew by Haim Watzman (London: Penguin, 2016).

Hanieh, Adam, *Lineages of Revolt: Issues of Contemporary Capitalism in the Middle East* (London: Haymarket Books, 2013).

Harms, Gregory and Ferry, Todd, *The Palestinian–Israeli Conflict* (London: Pluto, 2017).

Hass, Amira, *Drinking the Sea at Gaza: Days and Nights in a Land Under Siege* (New York: Henry Holt and Company, 1999).

Herzog, Chaim, *The Arab-Israeli Wars: War and Peace in the Middle East* (London: Arms and Armour Press, 1982).

Hodgkin, E.C. (ed.), *Letters from Palestine, 1932–36* (London: Quartet Books, 1986).

Khalidi, Rashid, *The Iron Cage: The Story of the Palestinian Struggle for Statehood* (London: Oneworld Publications, 2015).

Khalidi, Rashid, *The Hundred Years' War on Palestine* (London: Profile Books, 2020).

Kimmerling, Baruch, *Politicide: Ariel Sharon's War Against the Palestinians* (London: Verso, 2003).

Kimmerling, Baruch and Migdal, Joel, *The Palestinian People: A History* (London: Harvard University Press, 2003).

Kramer, Gudrun, *A History of Palestine* (Oxford: Princeton University Press, 2011).

Lockman, Zachary, and Beinin, Joel (eds.), *Intifada: The Palestinian Uprising Against Israeli Occupation* (Boston: South End Press, 1989).

Macintyre, Donald, *Gaza: Preparing for Dawn* (London: Oneworld, 2017).

Masalha, N., *Expulsion of the Palestinians* (Washington DC: Institute for Palestine Studies, 1992).

Masalha, N., *Imperial Israel and the Palestinians* (London: Pluto Press, 2000).

Matar, Dina, *What it Means to be Palestinian: Stories of Palestinian Statehood* (London: IB Taurus, 2011).

McHugo, John, *A Concise History of the Arabs* (London: Saqi, 2014).

Morris, Benny, *The Birth of the Palestinian Refugee Problem, 1947–1949* (Cambridge, UK: Cambridge University Press, 1988).

Morris, Benny, *Righteous Victims: A History of the Zionist–Arab Conflict, 1881–1999* (London: John Murray, 1999).

Morris, Benny (ed.), *Making Israel* (Michigan: University of Michigan Press, 2007).

Nathan, Susan, *The Other Side of Israel: My Journey Across the Jewish-Arab Divide* (London: Harper, 2006).

Nusseibeh, Sari, *Once Upon a Country: A Palestinian Life* (London: Halban, 2007).

Ophir, Adi, Givoni, Michal and Hanafi, Sari (eds.), *The Power of Inclusive Exclusion: The Anatomy of Israeli Rule in the Occupied Palestinian Territories* (New York: Zone Books, 2009).

Oppenheim, Walter, *The Middle East* (Simon & Schuster Education, 1989).

Ovendale, Ritchie, *The Origins of the Arab-Israeli Wars* (Harlow: Pearson, 1999).

Pappe, Ilan, *A History of Modern Palestine* (Cambridge, UK: Cambridge University Press, 2004).

Pappe, Ilan, *The Ethnic Cleansing of Palestine* (Oxford: Oneworld, 2007).

Porath, Y., *The Emergence of the Palestinian-Arab Nationalist Movement, 1918–1929* (London: Frank Cass, 1974).

Rogan, Eugene and Shlaim, Avi (eds.), *The War for Palestine: Rewriting the History of 1948* (Cambridge, UK: Cambridge University Press, 2001).

Rynhold, Jonathan, *The Failure of the Oslo Process: Inherently Flawed or Flawed Implementation?* (Israel: Begin-Sadat Center for Strategic Studies, Bar-Ilan University, 2008).

Said, Edward, *The End of the Peace Process: Oslo and After* (London: Granta Books, 2000).

Sayigh, Rosemary, *Palestinians: From Peasants to Revolutionaries* (London: Zed Books, 2013).

Sayigh, Yezid, *Armed Struggle and the Search for State: The Palestinian National Movement, 1949–1993* (Oxford, UK: Oxford University Press, 1997).

Scott-Baumann, Michael, *The Middle East, 1908–2011* (London: Hodder Education, 2016).

Segev, Tom, *One Palestine, Complete* (London: Abacus, 2000).

Segev, Tom, *1967: Israel, the War and the Year that Transformed the Middle East* (London: Little, Brown, 2007).

Shafir, Gershon, *A Half Century of Occupation: Israel, Palestine and the World's Most Intractable Problem* (Berkeley: University of California Press, 2017).

Shapira, Anita, *Israel: A History* (London: Weidenfeld and Nicolson, 2014)

Shavit, Ari, *My Promised Land: The Triumph and Tragedy of Israel* (London: Scribe, 2014).

Shehadeh, Raja, *Palestinian Walks: Notes on a Vanishing Landscape* (London: Profile Books, 2007).

Shehadeh, Raja, *Strangers in the House: Coming of Age in Occupied Palestine* (London: Profile Books, 2009).

Shehadeh, Raja, *Occupation Diaries* (London: Profile Books, 2013).

Shehadeh, Raja, *Language of War, Language of Peace: Palestine, Israel and the Search for Justice* (London: Profile Books, 2015).

Shindler, Colin, *A History of Modern Israel* (Cambridge, UK: Cambridge University Press, 2013).

Shlaim, Avi, *The Iron Wall: Israel and the Arab World* (London: Penguin, 2000).

Shlaim, Avi, *Israel and Palestine: Reappraisals, Revision, Refutations* (London: Verso, 2009).

Smith, Charles D., *Palestine and the Arab-Israeli Conflict* (Boston: Bedford/St. Martin's, 2007).

Usher, Graham, *Dispatches from Palestine: The Rise and Fall of the Oslo Peace Process* (London: Pluto Press, 1999).

Waxman, Dov, *The Israeli-Palestinian Conflict: What Everyone Needs to Know* (Oxford, UK: Oxford University Press, 2019).

Weizman, Eyal, *Hollow Land: Israel's Architecture of Occupation* (London: Verso, 2007).

Yiftachel, Oren, *Ethnocracy: Land and Identity Politics in Israel/Palestine* (Philadelphia: University of Pennsylvania Press, 2006).

Zertal, Idith, and Eldar, Akiva, *Lords of the Land: The War Over Israel's Settlements in the Occupied Territories, 1967–2007* (New York: Nation Books, 2007).

Online Sources

Arafeh, Nur, "50 Years of Occupation: Ongoing Colonial Economic Domination" (2017, accessed June 27, 2018), thisweekinpalestine.com/50-years-occupation-2.

Hanieh, Adam, "The Oslo Illusion" (2013, accessed July 16, 2018), jacobinmag.com/2013/04/the-oslo-illusion.

Ranta, Ronald, "Wasted Decade: Israel's Policies toward the Occupied Territories 1967–1977." Unpublished PhD thesis (accessed June 18, 2018), discovery.ucl.ac.uk/19038.

Journal and Newspaper Articles

Arnon, Arnie. 2007 "Israeli Policy Towards the Occupied Palestinian Territories: The Economic Dimension, 1967–2007," *Middle East Journal* 61, no. 4 (2007).

Aronson, Geoffrey, "Settlement Expansion as a National Enterprise," *Journal of Palestine Studies* 34, no. 4 (2005): 169–74.

Hanieh, Adam, "Development as Struggle: Confronting the Reality of Power in Palestine," *Journal of Palestine Studies* 45, no. 4 (2016): 32–47.

Karmi, Ghada, "Constantly Dangled, Endlessly Receding," *London Review of Books* 41, no. 23 (2019).

Rabbani, Mouin, "Palestinian Authority, Israeli Rule: From Transitional to Permanent Arrangement," *Middle East Report* 201 (1996): 2–6.

Rabinowitz, Dan, "Belated Occupation, Advanced Militarisation: Edward Said's Critique of the Oslo Process Revisited," *Critical Inquiry* 31, no. 2 (2005): 505–11.

Shikaki, Khalil, "The Peace Process, National Reconstruction, and the Transition to Democracy in Palestine," *Journal of Palestine Studies* 25, no. 2 (1996), 5–20.

Shlaim, Avi, "It's now clear: the Oslo peace accords were wrecked by Netanyahu's bad faith," *The Guardian*, September 12, 2013.

Thrall, Nathan, "Israel-Palestine: the real reason there's still no peace," *The Guardian*, May 16, 2017.

Image Credits

Maps on pp. 26, 41, 44, 65, 76, 88, 106, 159, and 192 courtesy of the author

p. 8: American Colony (Jerusalem) Photo Department, "Peasant family of Ramallah," Library of Congress

p. 10: Bettmann/Getty Images

p. 12: Carl Pietzner

p. 23: Hugo Mendelson, "President Chaim Weizman," 1949, National Photo Collection of Israel, Government Press Office

p. 28: American Colony (Jerusalem) Photo Department, "Arab protest delegations, demonstrations and strikes against British policy in Palestine (subsequent to the foregoing disturbances [1929 riots]). His Eminence the Grand Mufti of Jerusalem. Haj Amin Effendi el-Husseini," Library of Congress

p. 31: E. D. Robinson, "David Ben-Gurion, Chairman of the Jewish Agency Executive, delivers a speech at a public forum during an official visit to the Zeilsheim displaced persons camp," 1946, © United States Holocaust Memorial Museum, courtesy of Alice Lev

p. 32: "My name is Israel I am 20," National Library of Israel, Marvin G. Goldman EL AL Collection

p. 39: Unknown author via Wikimedia Commons

p. 45: Khalil Raad via Wikimedia Commons

p. 51: Mohamed Ali Eltaher via Wikimedia Commons

p. 61: Unknown author via Wikimedia Commons

p. 62: James Pringle/AP/Shutterstock

p. 63: World History Archive/Alamy

p. 69: Pictures from History/CPA Media Pte Ltd/Getty Images

p. 82: World History Archive/Alamy

p. 95: Keystone Press/Alamy

p. 99: Unknown author via Wikimedia Commons

p. 102: Fritz Cohen, "Sidewalk café on Ibn Gabirol Street, Tel Aviv," 1970, National Photo Collection of Israel, Government Press Office

p. 113: David Rubinger, "Paratroopers at the Western Wall," 1967, National Photo Collection of Israel, Government Press Office

p. 119: Moshe Milner, 1979, National Photo Collection of Israel, Government Press Office

p. 129: United Nations Relief and Works Agency for Palestine Refugees in the Near East (UNRWA), 1967

p. 133: atphalix via Wikimedia Commons

p. 135: Unknown author via Wikimedia Commons

p. 141: Castro/AP/Shutterstock

p. 144: Alex Levac

p. 153: Vince Musi, White House

p. 158: Reuters/Alamy

p. 166: Xinhua/Alamy

p. 168: Reuters/Alamy

p. 174: Ralph Alswang, White House

p. 186: Eddie Gerald/Alamy

p. 191: Ammar Awad/Reuters/Alamy

p. 197: Ismael Mohamad/UPI/Alamy

p. 203: Gin Kai, United States Navy

p. 217: Debbie Hill/UPI/Alamy

p. 218: US Embassy Jerusalem, "President Trump at the Israel Museum," 2017

p. 229: Yousef Masoud/Majority World CIC/Alamy

Acknowledgements

My thanks are due to the many people who have read and commented on parts or all of the text. They are Andy Baumann, Chris Beal, Professor Mary Embleton, Annie Evans, Sir Vincent Fean, Dr. Alec Hamilton, Tim Llewellyn, John McHugo, Miranda Pinch, Dr. Roy Sloan, Professor Roger Spooner, Professor Adam Sutcliffe, Roger Symon, Hannah Weisfeld, Bob Wolfson, and, above all, my most challenging and inspiring reader, Alison.

Thanks also to Laura Perehinec, publishing director at The History Press, who received my proposal and early draft with such enthusiasm, and Simon Wright and Alex Boulton, who guided me, and the book, through to completion.

Above all, I am indebted to Anna Bliss, of The Experiment Publishing, whose close reading and collaboration in preparing the US edition has been hugely appreciated.

Index

About the Author

MICHAEL SCOTT-BAUMANN is a graduate of Cambridge University and has an MA from the School of Oriental and African Studies in London. He has thirty-five years' experience as a history teacher and lecturer. He has travelled widely in the Middle East and conducted field work in the West Bank on Palestinian human rights. He lives in Cheltenham, England.